PARADISE LOST

Margarita Stocker

MACMILLAN

First published 1988

Published by
Higher and Further Education Division
MACMILLAN PUBLISHERS LTD
Houndmills, Basingstoke, Hampshire RG21 2XS
and London
Companies and representatives
throughout the world

Typeset by Wessex Typesetters
(Division of The Eastern Press Ltd)
Frome, Somerset

Printed in Hong Kong

British Library Cataloguing in Publication Data
Stocker, Margarita
    Paradise lost.—(The Critics debate).
    1. Milton, John, *1608–1674* Paradise lost
    I. Title   II. Milton, John, *1608–1674*.
    Paradise lost   III. Series
    821'.4   PR3562
ISBN 0–333–38442–3
ISBN 0–333–38443–1 Pbk

THE CR

General Editor: Michael Scott

Contents

General Editor's Preface

OVER THE last few years the practice of literary criticism has become hotly debated. Methods developed earlier in the century and before have been attacked and the word 'crisis' has been drawn upon to describe the present condition of English Studies. That such a debate is taking place is a sign of the subject discipline's health. Some would hold that the situation necessitates a radical alternative approach which naturally implies a 'crisis situation'. Others would respond that to employ such terms is to precipitate or construct a false position. The debate continues but it is not the first. 'New Criticism' acquired its title because it attempted something fresh, calling into question certain practices of the past. Yet the practices it attacked were not entirely lost or negated by the new critics. One factor becomes clear: English Studies is a pluralistic discipline.

What are students coming to advanced work in English for the first time to make of all this debate and controversy? They are in danger of being overwhelmed by the cross-currents of critical approaches as they take up their study of literature. The purpose of this series is to help delineate various critical approaches to specific literary texts. Its authors are from a variety of critical schools and have approached their task in a flexible manner. Their aim is to help the reader come to terms with the variety of criticism and to introduce him or her to further reading on the subject and to a fuller evaluation of a particular text by illustrating the way it has been approached in a number of contexts. In the first part of the book a critical survey is given of some of the major ways the text has been appraised. This is done sometimes in a thematic manner, sometimes according to various 'schools' or 'approaches'. In the second part the authors provide their own appraisals of the text from their stated critical standpoint, allowing the reader the knowledge of their own particular approaches from which their views may in turn be evaluated. The series therein hopes to introduce and to elucidate criticism of authors and texts being studied and to encourage participation as the critics debate.

Michael Scott

Acknowledgements

I am very grateful to Jocelyn Price for reading parts of the text. Gordon Campbell, T. G. S. Cain, Ernst Honigmann and Helen Wilcox were generous with information and practical help. I am also grateful to my colleagues in the Renaissance Research group at Liverpool, and to those at Crewe and Alsager College, who provided much stimulating feedback to my paper on feminist approaches to Milton. Michael Scott has been the most patient of editors, my husband the most patient of unpaid helps.

Note on the text

For Milton's poems reference is to the one-volume edition by Douglas Bush, *The Portable Milton* (Harmondsworth, 1976). For Milton's other writings references are to the Bohn edition of *The Prose Works*, ed. J. A. St John *et al.*, 5 vols. (London, 1848–53). Marvell is quoted from *The Poems*, ed. H. M. Margoliouth *et al.*, 3rd edn. (Oxford, 1971); Dryden from *Of Dramatic Poesy*, ed. G. Watson, 2 vols. (London and New York, 1962); Johnson from *Lives of the Poets: A Selection*, ed. J. P. Hardy (Oxford, 1971); Clive James from *Glued to the Box* (London, 1983).

References to these texts, and to critical works, are given in square brackets. Critical works are cited by author and date of publication, with page references as appropriate. In cases where a critic named in a given section does not appear in the corresponding section of the References, consult the Index.

Part One
Survey

Introduction

IN April 1981 the television critic of *The Observer*, Clive James, described the launching of the space shuttle *Columbia*, which had been delayed for several days by a malfunction in one of its four computers. He fantasised that the computer's mind was on other things. Having processed tax returns for Pittsburgh, it moved on to cataloguing old Bing Crosby hits and 'counting all the cows in India'. The computer dragged itself back to the launch only after completing a 'digital rewrite of *Paradise Lost*' [1983, 180–81]. Apart from their massiveness and pointlessness, the computer's extramural activities evidently shared an incongruity with its high-tech environment. They are also all readily recognisable cultural symbols or 'signs'. In this respect *Paradise Lost* is a text representative of Western culture, an accepted 'classic' of English literature. Through the centuries it has been constantly reread and re-evaluated in ways which reflect the shifting attitudes and values of its readers. This has been at once the most admired and the most reviled of literary 'classics': no major text has been so strongly challenged by influential critics as this epic was in the mid-twentieth century, or so thoroughly defended. For this reason, no less than because the poem has never failed to speak to different generations in diverse ways, the controversial critical history of *Paradise Lost* involves not only the important issues raised by this problematic text but also, to a degree, the history of our own attitudes and their contemporary manifestations. Although it was written over 300 years ago, this epic is not so incongruous an object in the 1980s as James's joke might suggest. Not as yet digitally rewritten, like other major texts it can be subjected to linguistic analysis by computer.

The cultural centrality of *Paradise Lost* is at least partly owing to its formal character as an epic. As traditionally conceived, epic was the fullest literary expression of its time, place, and culture. In Milton's epic this ambition is further amplified by his topic, for the religious subject comprises such archetypal matters as innocence and experience, Heaven and Hell, good and evil, and God. Whether these are interpreted mystically, mythically or psychologically, the archetypes have exercised a compulsion upon readers' imaginations that reflects their fundamental roles in Western thought. According to Irene Samuel [1968, 236], as a representation 'specifically of man's conspiring to destroy his own happiness' *Paradise Lost* 'inevitably speaks more immediately and obviously than most narratives on what man's happiness consists in, what maintained it, what ends it'. For Frank Kermode the epic's emphasis is the reverse – a myth about the origin and the horror of death, such a basic human preoccupation that the poem embodies (paradoxically) '*life* in a great symbolic attitude' [1963, 86–7: my italics].

More recently, with the growth of new approaches to literature, the focus of criticism has shifted from the 'meaning' of *Paradise Lost* to its status as a 'core text' in our culture – that is, in our cultural institutions. To feminist critics, for example, the poem's existence as a classic text for study in universities is an instance of the way in which other texts, especially those by women, have been forgotten or ignored in favour of the 'great works'. They argue that such texts are evaluated by masculine principles, that even the notion of a hierarchy of literary texts is an instance of male patriarchal attitudes. Of this critique *Paradise Lost* is particularly susceptible because, in its portrait of 'God the Father' and of human society, this poem is itself a manifestation of that patriarchal ideology which still oppresses women.

This is a contemporary instance of the way in which readers' reception of *Paradise Lost* has been, ever since its publication in 1667, largely determined by the prevailing political and religious attitudes. While this is partly owing to the poem's subjects, it has much to do with fluctuating attitudes also to Milton the man. Until his death in 1674 Milton's reputation was determined by his record as a revolutionary in the period of the English Civil War rather than by his writings. His poetry was not celebrated, and his participation in the great pamphlet wars of the 1640s and 50s had made little impact [Parker, 1940]. After the restoration of the monarchy in 1660 his life was endangered by the fact that he had supported the execution of Charles I, and royalist writers abused as treacherous both the man and his works. It was only to be expected that, whatever the literary virtues of his major poem, it would go a-begging for praise in such a climate. Yet, even shortly after his death, major writers and critics of the age stated their conviction that *Paradise Lost* was the greatest poem of its age: an age on which these writers – Dryden and Marvell amongst them – have themselves conferred distinction in the eyes of modern readers. Despite the opposition of so influential a critic (in his day) as Thomas Rhymer, by 1700 *Paradise Lost* was essentially established in its reputation as a 'classic' text, a reputation confirmed in a series of papers by Addison published in the *Spectator* of 1712. So complete was Milton's literary victory that the eighteenth-century attitude to his work might well be described as close to idolatry [Thorpe, 1965]. For its literary critics, *Paradise Lost* was almost beyond praise. For the poets, Milton's style was a model to be emulated. Beyond these, the poem had a large popular readership. Such a consensus between the cultural institutions and the marketplace is remarkable. But it has often been said that Milton's considerable influence upon the practice of eighteenth-century poets effectively strangled them [e.g. Havens, 1922], and Keats's later wrestling with the Miltonic influence upon his *Hyperion* is notorious. When in 1779 Samuel Johnson had the temerity to criticise Milton's poems for major flaws, the Milton idolatry rocked Johnson's reputation rather than the poet's.

After such adulation reaction was inevitable. Johnson's attitude to Milton, both as man and as poet, was adversely affected by Johnson's own Tory and high Anglican views. To the Romantics Milton's revolutionary Puritanism spoke differently. For Wordsworth Milton's poetry was a literary expression of political advance, congruent with the Romantic poet's enthusiasm for the French Revolution. To Blake, however, Milton's revolutionary spirit required revision as well as emulation. In his reading of *Paradise Lost*, 'The reason Milton wrote in fetters when he wrote of Angels & God, and at liberty when of Devils & Hell, is because he was a true poet and of the

Devil's party without knowing it' (*The Marriage of Heaven & Hell*, note to plate 6). Known now as the 'Satanist' reading, this notion that Milton unconsciously subverted his own 'godly' intentions by portraying the Devil sympathetically took a while to catch on: it was, after all, unlikely to appeal to the denizens of Victorian culture. Indeed, before the rediscovery of Milton's prose work *De Doctrina Christiana* (Of Christian Doctrine) in 1825, there had been no reason to believe that Milton was consciously heretical either. Throughout the eighteenth century and well into the nineteenth, *Paradise Lost* had been regarded not only as a literary classic but also as an improving work of devotion for Christian readers of all denominations. Even after the publication of *De Doctrina* Victorian critics remained immune to religious problems in *Paradise Lost*. The standard view was that of such influential critics as John Ruskin: Milton's ideas were exclusively theological, and these so uncomplicated as to be frankly boring. What the Victorians valued was Milton's artistry, his sublimely grand style, although they rarely stooped to describing precisely what it consisted in. They were confident in an assumption that they had no reason to think required defence, which is always an obstacle to intelligent criticism. Even so, by the late nineteenth century the critical reaction was beginning to emerge into the light. The publication of David Masson's biography of Milton [1881–96], which portrayed him as a rigid, austere Puritan, adversely affected Milton's popular image. He was now regarded as an unpleasant individual as well as an unoriginal thinker.

Now that defence was required, it appeared in the peculiar form of Saurat [1925]. He recognised that, if Milton was to be seen as personally unattractive, at least the poet's distance from normality might be made interesting if he were portrayed as a radical and daring thinker, rather than 'a monument to dead ideas' [Raleigh, 1900]. In an attempt to counteract this version of a heretical Milton, while restoring to him some semblance of human attraction, critics like Greenlaw [1917] and Hanford [1966] presented Milton in a new light. Far from being a narrow Puritan, he was a representative Renaissance figure, a Christian humanist thinker comparable with, say, Spenser. It was a sign of the times, however, that in 1930 Tillyard should partly resurrect the Satanist Milton by contrasting the poem's

'unconscious' with its 'conscious meaning'. Partly because of a
new taste for symbolic, indirect poetry – associated particularly
with Ezra Pound and T. S. Eliot – and partly because of the
involvement of English writers of the 1930s with radical
causes like the struggle against Franco in Spain, the cultural
moment was ripe for an unprecedented assault upon Milton's
eminent place in English literature. Indeed, there has been, in
our century, no comparable attack of such force, by critics of
such considerable influence, upon any other 'classic' writer.
When he launched what became known as the Milton
Controversy in 1936, Eliot's influence as a poet-critic was at its
apogee. He derogated Milton's style, the pernicious influence
of which upon English poetry must now be recognised: no
modern poet could or should learn from Milton. Equally,
Milton's religious ideas were repugnant. To second Eliot came
a critic whose ideas and practice were to affect the study of
English for decades, and whose influence is only now beginning
to recede. F. R. Leavis described Milton's verse as suffering
from the tyranny of sound over sense, as essentially unEnglish,
unintelligent, and musically monotonous. He confidently
pronounced Milton's reputation dead, and the burial effected
with 'remarkably little fuss' [1936/72, 46]. He was remarkably
wrong.

    Far from expiring quietly, *Paradise Lost* has continued to
evoke discussion from all quarters. Its defence against the
charges of Eliot, Leavis, and the neo-Satanist Waldock [1947]
burgeoned, after the neo-Christian reading of C. S. Lewis
[1942], into a major critical enterprise to rehabilitate the text
for modern readers. Apart from the more traditional, 'liberal
humanist' criticism of Milton written from the 1940s onwards,
Milton's epic has consistently attracted interpreters from the
newer schools of criticism which have emerged since the 1960s.
Because of the issues it raises, both as a text and as a cultural
'sign', *Paradise Lost* has been read in innumerable ways, a
diversity testifying to its continuing relevance. As in the past,
Milton's epic is now interpreted in ways that reflect the current
issues and anxieties of its readers.

    For this reason, and because the early Milton Controversy
has been described in detail elsewhere [Adams, 1955; Murray,
1967], in the critical survey which forms Part One of this book
I shall be most concerned to discuss more recent readings of the

poem. These include generic, political-historical, Marxist, archetypal, psychoanalytic, reader-oriented and feminist approaches. Each of these has something to tell us about Milton's text, even though their disagreements might suggest that to accept one is to reject the others. I do not propose to adjudicate between them, although I shall suggest the strengths and weaknesses of individual readings; their diversity is intrinsically interesting and suggestive. In Part Two, I shall be working from the theory of literary reception itself, in order to extrapolate from the 'reading history' of *Paradise Lost* one way in which we can interpret it now. Both Parts are concerned with the history of *Paradise Lost* as a text, and each aims to reflect its provocative variety. Generally speaking, those who read this poem for the first time are conditioned to approach it with fear and loathing. Neither is called for. Whatever the angle of view, *Paradise Lost* is a fascinating work.

Thematic approaches

What is *Paradise Lost* about? According to Tillyard, 'the question has by no means been settled' [1930, 237], nor is it now. Not only the answers, but the very formulation of the question, depend upon fundamental issues of literary theory. One could say that the difference between Samuel's answer and Kermode's (see Introduction) involves how one reads the title. Samuel is emphasising 'Paradise' and happiness, Kermode underlining 'Lost' and hence deprivation and death. This is not merely a subjective judgement, but a question of literary ideology. Reacting particularly to Kermode, Dyson and Lovelock [1973, 238–9] describe the great divide in literary criticism: one either believes 'that truth itself is relative', or one does not. Broadly speaking, 'liberal humanist' critics assume that literature reflects or at least attempts to express certain verities about human life. Literary consequences of this view include a conviction that, with due attention and adequate information, we can discover the 'essential meaning' of a text, and that this corresponds to the author's intention in writing it. Some classic assumptions were challenged before deconstruction affected criticism, as for instance by Wimsatt and Beardsley in their attack on 'the intentional fallacy' [1954].

They argued that, whether or not we can reconstruct an author's intention, it has no relevance to criticism of a text, for the text constitutes its own totality. As D. H. Lawrence said, it is the tale not the teller that we must believe. For critics of a sceptical temper that notion of belief is precisely what is questionable in liberal humanist approaches, for the latter assume that literature's 'verities' are capable of enlightening or improving the reader. Their opponents espouse a thoroughgoing version of that sceptical tradition of modern thought which draws upon Nietzsche, Marx and Freud.

Yet that tradition is so pervasive in twentieth-century thought that even some 'liberal humanist' critics manifest its tendencies. Tillyard in 1930 was already scornful of the old-fashioned 'simple-mindedness' that could believe Milton's own announcement of his poem's subject [237], which will 'assert Eternal Providence, / And justify the ways of God to men' [i 1–26]. Denying intentionalism, Tillyard is nevertheless concerned with the 'real' (that is, unconscious) subject of the poem. This is actually a rather unsceptical procedure. What mystic power confers upon Tillyard special access to Milton's unconscious? It could equally be argued that it is 'simple-minded' to assume a progressive model of history, in which we are wiser than our forebears because we know about Freud; that, also, we know better than Milton what the subject of his poem was. Their opponents often accuse liberal humanist critics of didacticism, of assuming an authority to tell readers what they ought to think. There is something in this, but the sceptics could also be said to lack humility, since they are busy correcting Milton as well as their opponents. They are as capable of dogmatism as liberal humanists. All literary criticism is ideological, but the merits and demerits of individual ideologies are in the eye of the beholder. Beholders are ideologues too.

The effect of liberal humanist ideology upon the interpretation of *Paradise Lost* can be seen not only in Christian readers like C. S. Lewis, but also in those critics who profess merely to place Milton in the history of ideas. Greenlaw, Hanford, Mahood [1917; 1966; 1950] and others reconstructed a 'Christian Humanist' Milton from Renaissance ideas, but the aim of this scholarly investigation was to make Milton a more amenable figure for the liberal humanist critics and readers of our own century. Modern humanism in this sense is a rather vague clutch of civilising principles, whereas Renaissance humanism derived from a systematic conflation of the classical philosophy of Plato with contemporary theology. Out of the Florentine tradition (especially from Marsilio Ficino) and through the influence of Erasmus and other religious reformers, humanism came to England relatively late, remaining influential in the earlier seventeeth century. In Milton's treatise *Of Education* his ideal syllabus for schoolboys (girls' education was considered unimportant) manifests a classic humanist emphasis upon the morally improving and civilising effect of learning, especially that which combined knowledge of the best Graeco-Roman writers with Christian principles. Such notions are still relevant because it is precisely the modern version of humanist education which is under attack in Thatcher's Britain, where study of the 'Humanities' is considered marginal. But if the humanist version of Milton retains interest, it is questionable whether Milton was especially humanistic for his time. The ideas cited to characterise Christian humanism in *Paradise Lost* are commonplaces, and though this makes their presence in the poem plausible, it also suggests that Milton is not necessarily emphatic about them – they may just be generalities of the poem's cultural milieu rather than vital to its subject.

As a Christian poem in classical epic form, *Paradise Lost* seems to reflect the humanist fusion of Christian with classical learning. Its assertion of man's free will can be regarded as humanist particularly when compared with Milton's *Areopagitica*, where liberty of thought and the growth of learning are regarded as contributing to mankind's progressive enlightenment. Similarly, the poem's stress upon reason as man's inner guide to the proper use of his freedom reflects the idea that reason was God's imprint upon the human mind, an intellectual conscience. This too has a context in Renaissance humanistic thought [Hoopes, 1962]. If Milton is regarded as a Christian humanist in very much the same manner as Spenser, one can conclude from its recommendation that passion be controlled by reason that *Paradise Lost* has more to do with Greek philosophy than with Genesis, despite the fact that Milton's story is the Genesis myth. On this basis Greenlaw [1917] argues that Adam's Fall occurs when passion conquers reason, temperance (in the Spenserian sense, that the way of Christian virtue eschews both asceticism and excess) being the poem's true theme. For this reading the apple has to be reduced to an empty symbol. If we accepted the apple as presented in the poem – the forbidden thing, which to eat is 'Disobedience' – we would be more interested in the religious meaning of Genesis than in the behavioural topic of temperance. For there is in fact an implicit opposition between the humanist Milton and the religious Milton, which becomes clear in Willey [1934; cf. Schultz, 1955; Svendsen, 1956]. The humanist version of Milton renders him attractively modern by aligning him with the Renaissance thirst for knowledge and rise of individualism. The notion that man could develop his own capacities to the utmost had its difficulties, for the Dr Faustus of the Renaissance could easily cross the invisible line between aspiration and a demonic egotism which repeats the original sin of pride. According to Willey, Milton fell foul precisely of this problem because he believed in liberty and the pursuit of knowledge. Since he also believed in God's authority over man, liberty was for him problematically restricted. He must deplore the disobedience of the Fall, but this very act in which Adam and Eve choose knowledge over obedience is 'the birth . . . of [man's] capacity for true "liberty"' [229]. This contradiction Milton cannot resolve, nor convince us that the Fall was malignant [230]. So if Milton did intend to justify God, he failed; if his true allegiance was to man's aspirations, he succeeded at the cost of self-contradiction. In either case, the poem is fundamentally flawed. But we need accept Willey's view only if we agree that Milton's humanism is more important than his theology.

His theology is in question, too. Is Milton orthodox or heretical? The humanist version of Milton is intended to get rid of theology as far as possible, by aligning him with secularly acceptable humanism and absorbing him into his period, hence contradicting the notion that Milton was a Puritan of a kind which distanced him from much Renaissance culture, and from us. Since modern liberal humanist critics usually find Puritanism unattractive, even those who think his theology vital to the poem have often chosen rather to emphasise Milton's congruence with traditional Christian thought. Finding that Milton's heterodox *De Doctrina* was reflected in the doctrinal ideas of *Paradise Lost*, Kelley [1941] challenged this view. The prose work shows, for instance, that Milton's notion of free will is Arminian, i.e. contradicting the Calvinist belief in God's predestination of a limited number of elect souls, and allowing the salvation of all who truly desire righteousness. God's statement that mankind shall be 'saved who will' (III 173–5] seems to imply that grace is available to all, not just to the elect. Yet, as Danielson – who also thinks Milton Arminian – notes, God later refers to souls 'Elect above the rest' [III 184; Danielson, 1982, 82]. He thinks that Milton is attempting a compromise between Arminian and Calvinist doctrines here, even though these were antagonistic and hotly argued in the mid-seventeenth century [58–83]. This suggestion is plausible if we recall that for two centuries readers failed to notice heresy in *Paradise Lost*. Patrides [1966] portrays it as traditional at least in Protestant terms; Christopher [1982] argues for an especially Reforming – Lutheran and Calvinist – orthodoxy in Milton. We might well conclude that Milton was careful to address most Protestant readers, even if this meant underplaying or obscuring his personal inflections of traditional belief.

There is, however, at least one evident doctrinal issue in *Paradise Lost*: the Son's relationship to God. The Arian heresy, which seems to be present in *De Doctrina*, denied divinity to the Son and therefore posited an essential difference between God and Christ. Crucially affecting the doctrine of the Trinity, Arianism could be detected for instance in Milton's emphasis upon God's elevation of the Son, which tends to imply that hitherto the Son had not been recognised in Heaven as specially related to God, still less 'part of God'. On the other hand, it has been argued against the Arian view upheld by Kelley that the heresy involved is subordinationist (i.e. that the Son is simply subordinate to the Father), a much less radical position [Hunter, Patrides and Adamson, 1971]. The controversy here has literary implications when we ponder the fact that in the poem's terrestrial episodes God appears only in the form of the Son; and the Son is portrayed as implementing the earthly Creation. Both of these suggest God's inaccessibility from the earthly plane, and hence might imply that the Son does not possess the same transcendent divinity even before he becomes incarnate in man. If so, Milton is further underlining the Son's mediate relationship between God and man, bringing him in effect (relatively speaking) closer to man than he might otherwise be.

Such matters are fraught with theological niceties, and most readers could well do without them. Even discounting Milton's heresy, however, *Paradise Lost* has overt theological problems. Almost no-one has a good word for Milton's God, and Satan has often been regarded as his most successful character. Most influential of the new Satanists was Waldock [1947], who went further than Tillyard's contention that Satan represented something Milton himself could not resist, 'heroic energy' [1930, 277]. For Waldock, Milton's God was so nasty, his elevation of the Son so needlessly provocative, that Satan's complaint of divine tyranny appeared reasonable. To make Satan seem a worthy opponent for the Omnipotent, Milton had to allow him at least the semblance of heroism, might, and a plausible grudge. By the time this heroic portrait is corrected – in Satan's self-condemning soliloquy [IV 32–113] it is too late, for the reader's view is fixed. In Waldock's analysis Milton bit off more than he could chew. Attempting to present God 'frontally' (unlike Dante, who never lets us 'see' God), Milton inevitably made his seem inhuman: after all, by definition God is not human. When anthropomorphic characteristics are attributed to him (an inevitable result of trying to portray him at all), his apparent vindictiveness makes things worse [e.g. III 80ff.]. Between this God and this Satan, Milton's attempt to 'justify' God lies in ruins, for he is neither just nor merciful. Actually, almost everything Waldock says is questionable, especially his assumption that he somehow knows what 'we' think at any given point. His argument about God has more basis, however, and while few of Waldock's opponents cared to defend this God, Empson [1961] was able to press the attack. He argues that Milton insists that God intended the Fortunate Fall. Since the Fall is Satan's objective too, God can hardly be regarded as better; or as anything but capricious to condemn Satan for doing his dirty work for him [39]. Empson does not see this cruel God as a flaw. On the contrary, he considers the Christian God 'wicked' anyway, and in so far as Milton struggles to make him more acceptable the poet is to be congratulated for contradicting his theological beliefs. Empson is confident that the charges laid against *Paradise Lost* thus

indicate the very things that 'make the poem good' [10–11].
Is it in fact the case that Milton's subject is the Fortunate
Fall? Is this the only way to 'justify' God? Assumptions about
the Fortunate Fall are widespread in Milton criticism,
especially as influenced by Lovejoy [1937]. At what is taken to
be a climax in the poem, Adam rejoices 'That [God] all this
good of evil shall produce, / And evil turn to good' [xii 464–71].
He is assured by Michael that, in place of Eden, Adam shall
experience 'A Paradise within thee, happier far' [587]. The
fortunate outcome shows that God is good and everything will
be all right in the end. Yet, as we see in Empson, the Fortunate
Fall notion lays God's goodness open to challenge. Milton's
competence is challengeable too. Why does he spend two books
telling Adam (and us) how woeful life will be after the Fall
[xi–xii], if he is promulgating this optimistic moral? Not
surprisingly, accepting the Fortunate Fall premise, Marshall
[1965] finds that the last two books are an anticlimax. Till then
Milton had implied the Fortunate perspective indirectly,
especially by his ironic treatment of Satan. We know that his
success against Adam and Eve is temporary, and this makes for
a dramatic tension and emotional involvement on the reader's
part. After the Fall, however, Milton can only insist on what we
know already, by intellectual rather than dramatic
demonstration. Indeed, Marshall doubts whether the two
subjects – Disobedience and Justification – can be successfully
brought together at all. In his dislike of the final books he is
representative of those who adopt the Fortunate view. That
vigorous defender of the poem, Lewis, found them distasteful
too.

On the other hand, what if these critics' desire to read
Milton's God and his theology 'positively' is misleading them?
Certainly some Calvinists of Milton's day believed not only
that the Fall was Fortunate, but that therefore God actually
predestined it. (Shades of Empson's wickedly unfair God here.)
If, however, Milton was an Arminian he could not have
accepted this notion while retaining his belief in man's free will,
a belief which the epic constantly reiterates. Adam and Eve
were 'free to fall', not pushed [iii 99]. Logically, as Danielson
[1982] suggests, Milton was much more likely to have regarded
the Fall as unfortunate. God says as much: 'Happier, had it
sufficed [man] to have known / Good by itself, and evil not at

all' [xi 88–9]. If mankind had the option to remain happy, and chose not to, then God was indeed merciful to restore them to another form of happiness in the end. Danielson argues that the option – to resist temptation – is evident in Abdiel, the one angel who resisted Satan's subornation. So Milton has already, in Book V, shown us the alternative to what happens in Book ix. If the Fall was unfortunate, an irrecoverable loss no matter what else man is given in its place, then it is indeed tragic that he knows evil because it was unnecessary. That tragedy is, then, successfully presented as the great 'Woe' of Books xi–xii. Such a view has the virtue of being at once a literary explanation for Milton's final books, and a theological explanation of considerably more sophistication than the Fortunate Fall. The 'Lost' in Milton's title would mean precisely that. If Milton's subject is justification of God and the explanation of evil – that is, theodicy – he faces both theological and literary problems [Stocker, 1987]. Those problems might well be more adequately answered by the Unfortunate Fall.

Was Milton's Eden really such a great loss? The Edenic myth 'yearned, as no Milton could, for the blank innocence and effortlessness of a golden age' [Willey, 229; Waldock, 22]. Certainly Milton regarded trial and temptation as proper to the wayfaring Christian, and was no enthusiast for 'cloister'd virtue'. It follows for Willey that Adam and Eve show sinful characteristics even before the Fall, for their absence would prevent moral choice [229]. Several critics agree in seeing Adam and Eve as 'fallen before the Fall', particularly in Adam's curiosity (rebuked by Rapael, viii 172–8) and Eve's dream, in which she seems to respond to the hubris (damnable pride) symbolised by flying with Satan [v 26–93]. But Waldock states in more basic terms what we might call the horticultural problem. Milton did not really believe in 'primal happiness', and the only thing he can find to occupy Adam and Eve is . . . gardening. Any normal person would regard this as 'an eternity of boredom' [125]. Actually, some people enjoy gardening (not I), but Waldock is as usual confident that he represents normality. More important, in his investigation of the traditional interpretations of Genesis that Milton inherited, Evans [1968] argues that Milton is unusual in taking the command to 'dress and keep' the garden so seriously. He gives it a vital symbolic function, representing the necessity for right reason to tame and order the passions. Prelapsarian virtues are not static; in order to *act* rightly Adam and 'Eve require guidance and self-control. Until enlightened, Eve is drawn more to her own reflection than to Adam. In Eve, Adam's control of his own passions is externalised: her hair is 'wanton' like the garden's growth, and she needs guidance equally as she is correct to argue that the garden needs pruning. Evans refers to the traditional marital symbols of the vine and the elm [IV 307, v 215–19] to show that Eve's flower-like nature [IX 432–3] reflects the garden itself, its beauties and its wildness. He also repeats the (widely accepted) view of Lewis, that the whole poem is based upon the ordered and ascending hierarchies of Creation [Lewis, 73–81]. Adam's place is below the angels, Eve's subordinate to Adam. Yet this placing is not static either: by means of rational self-development human beings can perfect themselves, fulfilling God's promise that unfallen humanity will eventually rise to the heavenly state [v 469–503, vII 156–9]. Milton's doctrine of human perfectibility is, then, the informing principle of Edenic happiness, which can change and develop [Evans, 244–71]. Lewalski [1969] argues that Adam and Eve are allowed to test and develop themselves in the garden without sin. In this light Eve's dream is an experience which, in their discussion of its significance, forwards ethical and intellectual growth.

As usual, arguments defending the text's success produce further difficulties. Evans's forthright statement of the hierarchical principle would, in a feminist view, add to the problems of Milton's God and Satan the problem of a misogynist version of Eve.

Form and genre

The Renaissance notion of hierarchies of being was replicated in their literary attitudes. Poetic 'kinds' or genres were ranged in ascending order from simple lyrics up to the highest, the 'heroic poem' or epic. To write epic was, precisely, to be the most heroic of literary practitioners. For Dryden 'A Heroic poem, truly such, is undoubtedly the greatest work which the soul of man is capable to perform' [1697, II 223]. Not surprisingly, in the Renaissance effort to emulate classical achievements the writing of a Christian epic was high on the agenda: it had to be the literary equal of Homer and Virgil while surpassing them in Christian 'truth' [see Greene, 1963]. Before Milton in England no poet had achieved this desirable fusion. Even Spenser's *Faerie Queene*, while inspirational for Milton, could be regarded as more romance than epic, and anyway it was unfinished. For many years Milton cast around for both a topic and a form for his major work, but his final determination upon a biblical subject in epic fulfilled at once his own ambitions and – as articulated by Sidney's *Defence of Poetry* [1595] – a national dream.

In the seventeenth century the most influential classical epic was the *Aeneid*. According to Lewis, it was Virgil who redirected 'Secondary Epic' into its crucial concern with history and national destiny, which Milton extends to comprise spiritual history [32–4]. The extent of Virgilian influence on *Paradise Lost* is well attested [Harding, 1962; Knott, 1971]. Yet in order to revise classical epic upon Christian lines Milton needed to re-evaluate the epic hero. Adam is not a warrior like Aeneas. To Dryden he could not be an epic hero because he was not victorious [II 233]. Johnson disputed that an epic hero should necessarily end in prosperity [102], although he agreed that Milton had thoroughly revised the rules of heroic poetry. Indeed, Dryden had doubted that *Paradise Lost* was classifiable in this way, since Milton's hero was not Adam but the Devil – thus launching the Satanist controversy long before Blake's provocative remark.

It is in the relative heroic stature of Satan, Adam, and Christ that Milton's epic innovations centre. Satan may appear heroic – and is constantly compared to Achilles and other classical heroes – but what he reflects is specifically their vainglorious and militaristic bent [Bowra, 1945; Steadman, 1967]. Amongst Miltonists there is broad agreement that Milton's use of classical parallels in the Satanic portrait is ironic. Important here is the common assumption that Milton rated military courage low compared to the spiritual warfare of the active Christian. In *Paradise Lost* he provides an explicit critique of classical epic values: 'in those days might only' was 'valor and heroic virtue called', and the 'infinite Manslaughter' of battle and pillage was 'held the highest pitch / Of human glory'. Meanwhile, 'what most merits fame [is] in silence hid' [XI

689–99]. That inner struggle with evil is what Milton aims to bring out of silence into epic expression.

Yet Waldock saw Milton's deepest attachments as inhering in Satan, who is admirable for 'fortitude . . . endurance . . . splendid recklessness [and] leadership' [77], especially in his rallying of the dejected fallen angels and his journey into the great Chaos. Steadman agrees about the fortitude, but thinks that it reflects ambivalence in the Renaissance attitude to the Ancients. Unaware of Christian revelation, their notions of heroism were limited to a 'Gentile virtue' which Satan also manifests [1968, 209–11]. After the Fall only Christ is capable of heroism in the true sense, a sense defined by Milton's mode of characterisation: 'character is inseparable from ethical decision' [1968, viii–x, 32]. So the epic narrative hinges upon that 'act of moral choice' which is the Fall, after which human heroism becomes possible only in imitation of Christ's great redemptive action. While Satan's expedition against mankind seems like a heroic mission of conquest (like that of Aeneas in Italy), by seventeenth-century Protestant standards it is self-glorifying and therefore decisively inferior to that which glorifies God [211]. Like Lewis, Steadman sees Satan's leadership as a matter of rhetorical cunning and the demonic council as sophistry in action [227f.]. His desperate 'Evil, be thou my Good' in the Niphates soliloquy [IV 110] signifies his personification of nonsense, that he is 'a Lie rather than a Liar' [Lewis, 94–5]. Rajan points out that Milton's contemporaries would have found Satan's talk of 'liberty' frankly amusing, coming from one they were accustomed to regard as the first liar [1947, 95–6].

This combination of Christian and classical motifs is seen as participating in Milton's 'conscious antithesis between true and illusory patterns' of heroism and kingship. Satan's is force without moral courage, deriving from both classical and scriptural sources. His vengefulness imitates Homer's Achilles, while his urge to usurp and conquer has biblical precedent in the giants of Genesis and in Nimrod – figures so characterised in book XI [Steadman, 1967, xviii]. Military valour is devalued in comparison to 'suffering for truth's sake / [which] Is fortitude to highest victory' [XII 569–70]. By such radical reassessments of heroic values Milton is seen to be redefining, revising, even perhaps 'refuting' epic in pure 'anti-epic'

[Hagin, 1964; Spencer, 1968; Kates, 1974]. Webber [1979] suggests that epic was usually subversive of accepted social values anyway, but Ryken thinks Milton goes further than his predecessors by rejecting the epic 'framework itself' [Sims and Ryken, 1984, 48n.].

Such epic revaluation was both demanded by Milton's belief and effected by reference to scriptural authority. The plot, of course, derives from Genesis, but a wide range of biblical echoes and allusions permeates *Paradise Lost*. From these Sims [1962] concludes that Milton intended his readers not only to recognise allusions but also to be subliminally affected by those which were not consciously recognised. This process affects even non-Biblical material, for Nyquist shows that Milton greatly expands the Genesis account of the Temptation dialogue between Eve and the Serpent, while remaining so close to its psychological and theological dynamics (as traditionally interpreted) that the reader does not notice his additions [1984, 215–23]. Milton's religious sources extend beyond the Bible itself to works in the hexameral tradition – i.e. those, like Du Bartas's *La Sepmaine*, which describe the six-day Creation of Genesis 1 – and Kurth [1959] has gone so far as to suggest that *Paradise Lost* is not epic but hexameron. I think, however, that we can take Milton's word for it that he set out to write a 'heroic poem' [*PL*, 'The Verse'].

More recently, attention has shifted from the 'influence' of the Bible to its status as an 'intertext' of *Paradise Lost*, especially in generic terms. In their anthology, Sims and Ryken [1984] are concerned not with sources and parallels so much as with the way this epic maintains a dialogue with scripture. Webber had claimed that in the Renaissance the Bible was itself regarded as an epic [1979, 157], but Ryken amplifies the point by suggesting that Milton saw the Bible as 'a model for literary form' across the broad range of genres [43], for all the kinds were thought to have come within its compass. Ryken argues that Milton 'killed' epic's heroic ethos by substituting for its military and glorious values domestic and pastoral values; for the theme of human greatness, divine greatness contrasting human littleness; for warfare and kingship their spiritualised alternatives. That transformation was effected by imitation of biblical models, drawn respectively from Genesis, Exodus and Revelation [45–6]. Focusing not on a battlefield but on the

paradisal life of Adam and Eve, *Paradise Lost*'s emphasis upon
the private makes it the first 'domestic epic'. Even the epic crisis
is 'a decidedly domestic act' [50], in which Adam chooses his
wife over obedience to God. Genesis has similarly domestic and
pastoral emphases. We might expect this, given that it is
Milton's source anyway, but Ryken has a real point to make –
that the heroes of Genesis are not socially elevated (as the
classical hero is), but 'family leaders and tillers of the soil' [52].
Such a humbly domestic focus, while foreign to classical epic, is
basic to the scriptural and spiritualised view. By intertextual
means the anthology generally is intended to revise the
prevailing view that Milton's literary models were classical,
while the Bible was a largely unliterary source affecting plot
and ideas; in fact it can be regarded as Milton's foremost
literary model [27].

Other studies have also reassessed Milton's deployment of
classical genres in his depiction of Paradise. In the
Renaissance, Virgil's progress from 'apprentice-work' in
pastoral genres to mature expression in epic was considered the
paradigm for an ambitious poetic career. Heroic poems often
contained pastoral episodes, evocations of a golden age of rural
pastimes and easy contentment, and in *Paradise Lost* Milton
draws upon both classical and Christian models for the lost age
of innocence [Giamatti, 1966; Knott, 1971]. In her study of
Milton's complex mixture of genres Lewalski suggests that he
imports georgic (the genre of rural labour, following Virgil's
Georgics) into Edenic pastoral. Adam and Eve's horticulture is
prelapsarian, easy work, in contrast to Virgil's hard-labouring
husbandmen. Since their gardening represents self-cultivation
this is a 'georgic of the mind' [1985, 196]. A similar argument is
offered by Low [1985, 310–18], who contrasts prelapsarian
pastoral with postlapsarian georgic, in that fallen Adam is
cursed with tilling the ground to survive [IV 327–31 contrasting
XI 261–2]. Low's thematic conclusion is that, since Eden was a
rather agricultural garden which included 'Fields' tended by
Adam and Eve, similarly their postlapsarian tillage represents
an ability to reattain Edenic perfection, although on harder
terms [317–9]. These genres combine with biblical models, the
episode of Eve's dream being modelled on the Song of Songs.
Its epithalamium, or wedding-song sequence, lies behind
Adam's dawn song, which the Tempter parodies in his

serenade to Eve [v 26–93, 17–25; ix 538–48]. The whole episode reflects in this first marriage the Song's paradigmatic relationship of Spouse to Bride [Lewalski, 1985, 201ff.]. Sacred and secular literary models thus reinforce each other.

In viewing Revelation as the inspiration for Milton's Christocentric spiritual epic, Ryken [1984, 79] builds upon critical work which has shown that this apocalyptic book was the epic *within* the Bible [Wittreich, 1977], and that it is crucial to Milton's [Fixler, 1964]. Revelation has the epic features of heroic conflict, epic catalogues, a mixture of genres from lyric to extended narrative, visions and an 'authoritative' writer [Wittreich, 1977]. However, Wittreich is concerned to deny that *Paradise Lost* is an epic, claiming it for the genre of 'prophecy'. Of course, apocalypse and prophecy are related, but there is no genre of 'prophecy'. Dobbins [1975] demonstrated echoes of Revelation (and its Reformation exegetes, especially David Pareus, whom Milton admired) in *Paradise Lost*, at their densest in the War in Heaven [v–vi]. Although Dobbins is a confusing guide, he makes his point that the War in Heaven is not in fact an episode determined solely by Milton's emulation of Homeric and Virgilian battles, but a rendition of the celestial conflict in Revelation 5 and 12. The suggestion that Revelation was Milton's literary model was contested by Patrides [1984], but as Ryken observes, Patrides is using the 'source/echo' test upon Revelation instead of seeing it as a literary model for Milton's epic techniques. Christ is his epic hero in the sense that he is Revelation's, 'who conquers his enemies and establishes his eternal empire' [Sims and Ryken, 1984, 76], that which is promised for the end of time. In that sense Revelation has already transformed for Milton the *Aeneid*'s theme, which was Aeneas's establishment of what would become the Roman Empire.

Revelation and classical epic share an aspiration to canvas the broadest reaches of space and time. Epic had, indeed, always required of its author an encyclopedic range, which is so fully achieved for its own time by *Paradise Lost* that Rajan can regard Milton 'as possibly the last person in history to hold all human knowledge for his province' [1947, 21]. Revelation's outreach to the furthest end of time, and the prophecy of ultimate happiness for humankind in Christ's Kingdom, provide evident warrant for Milton's 'world history' in the epic's final books [Fixler, 230–3]. Despite the happy end, Revelation also informs their tragic tone, for the biblical book was itself 'a high and stately tragedy' [Milton, *Prose*, II 479]. At one point in his meditations upon the right form for his theme, Milton had sketched out a classical tragic drama, *Adam Unparadised*. When he turned to epic, at least one fragment of the tragedy was incorporated into *Paradise Lost*: Satan's Niphates soliloquy. Its prior existence can be adduced to refute Waldock's notion that this was Milton's desperate remedy, having made Satan too attractive hitherto. Gardner [1965] notes that Satan is often portrayed dramatically in soliloquy, speculating that the device gives him an appeal similar to that of the tragic heroes of Elizabethan drama. Unlike its villains, figures like Macbeth evoke a complex of pity and condemnation to which Satan also lays claim.

Milton's hesitation between the two kinds was unsurprising, for Aristotle had considered them closely allied. A considerable portion of Milton criticism is devoted to such dramatic features, and the popular 1950s/60s view, that Milton makes much use of irony and indirection in the deployment of the poem's 'scenes' [Stein, 1953; Hanford, 1966], involves 'dramatic' assumptions. Indeed, Barker [1965] suggests that the ten-book division of the poem's first edition reflected its dramatic five-act structure, obscured in the final twelve-book version. There was in the seventeenth century a lively theoretical debate about the possible merger of theatrical and heroic forms, a merger which Demaray [1980] thinks fulfilled in *Paradise Lost*'s 'theatrical epic'. From Continental sources and English courtly masques Milton draws inspiration for a series of theatrical spectacles and triumphs, especially in the processional spectacle of world history which forms books XI–XII. In 'prophetic show' these enact Pareus's conviction that Revelation was a 'Prophetical Drama' [23]. But the opening books manifest the division of masque into main-masque and antimasque: the 'disorderly intrusion' of the latter occurring as the demonic conclave of book II, while in book III God presides over a masque of concord in which the angels' hymns replicate masque songs. This structural opposition imitates the staging of masques like Milton's own *Comus*, where the action occupies a central space (here, the earth) between two 'thrones', God's and Satan's [31–7]. Particular episodes also recall masques, as for example in Pandemonium's similarity to the fabulous palaces constructed for such spectacles as Davenant's *Britannia Triumphans* of 1637 [35–6; *PL* I 710–15]. While affecting its writing, theatrical devices are significant for our reading of the epic because Milton's 'verbal appeal to the theatrical arts' affects evaluation of its themes. Satan's various disguises – as cherub, serpent, demagogue – should affect our assessment of his role because they represent 'false, theatrical masks'. Upon accepting these at face value the Romantic misprision of Satan depended [61; cf. Waddington, 1962].

In XI–XII Sasek [1965] sees a similar dramatic lesson. Adam has yet to understand the Fall either intellectually or emotionally, so we see here not 'a mere historical pageant' but the spectacle of Adam undergoing vicarious suffering for the future consequences of his action. Whereas in classical epics and in Du Bartas such a vision was presented descriptively, Milton presents it dramatically, as an interactive dialogue between Michael and Adam. Throughout, Adam has a tendency to overreact which is repeatedly corrected by the angel until he finally reaches that state of balance between sorrow and hope which God intends [XI 117], and in which the epic closes. Dramatic presentation shows that XI–XII are part of the main plot rather than a loose extension of it, at once completing Adam's education and indicating his representation for humanity generally.

Movement to the relative optimism of this conclusion involves a shift from the tragic mood which Milton had announced at the beginning of book IX [5–6]. Stevenson [1984] sees that shift as effected within the ninth book itself, as it moves from the opening phrase 'No more' to the closing 'No end'. In the first is embodied the Fall's tragic loss, in the latter the possibility – 'of their vain contest [there] *appeared* no end' – of rescue from the misery of sin. Between these is performed a whole tragic drama, in which Adam, Eve, and Satan are role-playing antagonists [106]. Whether or not IX really does contain five 'acts', as Stevenson thinks, her view that tragedy is modified does, like other interpretations of Milton's dramatic devices, have implications for whether we view *Paradise Lost* as a divine *commedia* or a tragedy, and whether its subject is Fortunate or Unfortunate Fall.

The narrative in which that subject is embedded was for

Waldock the fundamental flaw. Unlike us, Milton had not acquired the narrative sophistication conferred by experience of the novel. Failing to recognise that the Genesis myth will not bear narrative amplification, Milton attempted to correct its antitheological tendencies by intrusive authorial statements. So, when Adam falls by love, evoking our sympathy, Milton hastily informs us that he is merely 'fondly overcome with female charm' [IX 999; Waldock, 22f.]. On such occasions Milton's 'allegations clash with his demonstrations' [78]. Surely, though, there is no necessary privileging in narrative of a character's speech over the narrative voice. Despite his apparent concern for narrative, Waldock is viewing the poem as if it were a play Milton was watching with us, 'pulling our sleeve' [77] the while. Perhaps this merely confirms Milton's effective use of dramatic devices!

Demaray sees their various manifestations as held together within the narrator's field of vision [1980, xv]. For Ferry the narrator *is* the epic's unity, his invocations opening books I, III, IV and IX deliberately maintaining our awareness that he is our guide [1963, 8–17]. Not Milton himself, the narrator is a projection whose constant reference to his conscious artistry underlies all his comments on the action. As a director, his statements always carry more authority than any character's [44–66]. An example is Satan's entry into Paradise: many critics assume that we (fallen readers) see it through Satan's eyes, sharing his alienation from a state we have lost. Yet, as Ferry demonstrates, the point of view here cannot be Satan's because the narration shifts perspectives above and beyond his vantage-point [51–4]. Ferry's argument that the invocations are the epic's centre of meaning is extended by Schindler's further emphasis upon the way in which Milton modelled them upon the psalms [1984]. To assume the divine inspiration of David's biblical poems buttresses the narrator's authority and matches his sacred theme with an appropriate scriptural model. In the light of the narrator's rejection of classical muses for the Muses of the Spirit [Sims and Ryken, 1984, 28], we can judge how far epic was transformed by Milton.

Historical approaches

Milton's revaluation of epic values is closely bound up with his revolutionary politics. While humanist critics tended to want to underplay his Puritanism, a movement to restore centrality to his religious and political aims has recently gathered momentum. In this context the crucial problem is that a professed revolutionary, supporting the execution of Charles I, should nevertheless in *Paradise Lost* condemn Satan as a rebel and endorse the unquestioned authority of Heaven's King [Ross, 1943]. Related to this ideological conundrum is the literary problem of the War in Heaven, which presents Satan's insurrection and Christ's victory. From Johnson onwards, critics have often found this episode a puzzling mixture of epic battle and risible hyperbole. The loyal angels' resort to mountain-tossing against their opponents made Waldock think that even Milton had to giggle at his fantasy [112; cf. Peter, 1960, 77]. However, Stein thought that the point here was precisely to burlesque militarism [1953, 20–3]; an apparently illogical suggestion, since it is unlikely that Milton would wish to ridicule the loyal angels at any rate. In the work of historical critics a very different picture emerges.

Considering *Paradise Lost* in the context of Civil War polemic, Whiting [1964] shows that the 'sons / Of Belial, flown with insolence and wine' [ɪ 501–2] are the Cavaliers as described in Puritan execrations, while the warrior angel Michael and his loyal cohorts reflect the Cromwellian army's self-image, as the Saints warring against the Dragon in God's own cause. Such ideas are deeply implicated in contemporary Puritan millenarianism, Milton himself being one of those who regarded the Saints as fighting to bring Christ's final Kingdom into being [Berry, 1976; Firth, 1979, 232–7; Fixler, 1964; Hill, 1977]. From this angle, Milton's apocalyptic description of Michael's combat with Satan [Dobbins, 1975] inhabits two time zones. In typological terms (the way an Old Testament event foreshadows a New Testament event), Madsen argues, this description of the first war between good and evil also prefigures the last apocalyptic conflict. That the conflict remains indecisive till Christ intervenes signifies the moral that godly saints who fight this battle on earth must bear with patience their frustration till the Second Coming, for Christ alone can conquer the forces of evil [1968, 85–111]. In Madsen's view this long perspective holds together the whole narrative of the poem, the War in Heaven being both a structural and a thematic centre. The twelve-book version makes the centrality of v–vi evident, i–iv showing evil in the ascendant while vii–xii evince a counter-emphasis upon Creation and recreation [Barker, 1965; cf. Shawcross, 1965]. Representing God's redemptive pattern, the War in Heaven is the poem's major image of providence [Summers, 1962, 112f.].

In this context it becomes clear that Satan is not an egalitarian revolutionary but a usurper, whose assertion of what he regards as the traditional hierarchy in Heaven against the Son's elevation produces parallels with the absolutist Charles I [Bennett, 1977]. Given his conviction that in the Civil War God was on the Parliamentarian side, after their defeat in the Restoration of 1660 Milton was faced with the problem of why their cause could possibly have failed, and 'tyranny' been reinstated in Charles II's government [Fixler, 1964]. Believing that Christ would literally reign upon earth, Milton was concerned to discover the right mode of political action to bring on his Kingdom. In retrospect, it was clear that godly revolution had been infected with men's own ambitious political delusions [223]. Therefore, in xi–xii, history is the chronicle of many and various trials testing men's obedience to God's will [xi 385–60]. Satan's original rebellion re-emerges in historical forms, like the tyranny of Nimrod. Such tyrannies collude with men's capacity for servitude, for they are generally ignorant of and unequal to the strenuous demands of liberty [xii 73–106; Fixler, 231–3]. This political aspect of fallen humanity evidently invites application to Milton's own time, when England voluntarily resubmitted herself to servitude under monarchy. Effectively politics and spirituality are compounded in an epic where Satan loses the Kingdom of Heaven, seeking a compensatory dominion in earth; whereas man loses to Satan the kingdom of paradise but ultimately reattains the Kingdom of Heaven through redemption by Christ the King [228]. In this way Fixler can resolve Milton's ideological conundrum, since unlike earthly monarchies 'Dominion and subjection . . . under the rule of *love*, are . . . reciprocal aspects' of God's Kingdom [230]. In defeat, Milton turns to the inward version of the Kingdom, the 'Paradise within' the individual [XII 587]; Fixler concluding, like Madsen, that Milton finally rejects political action in favour of patient waiting for the ultimate Kingdom to arrive [272–3].

Although Hill [1977] broadly agrees with Fixler's analysis of Milton's final resort to the internal paradise, as a Marxist he is concerned rather to highlight the contradictions in Milton's ideology than to resolve them. Like Milner [1979] and Hodge [1981], he reasserts the problems raised by Waldock and Empson. Finding that Milton was torn between respectable Puritan culture and that of the radical sects, Hill locates in his 'deeply divided personality' a reluctant but real attraction to the proto-communist radicals of the 1640s and 50s, despite his defence of more conservative programmes of reform [1977, 337–57]. That division informs his ambivalent treatment of Satan, whose 'Turkish despotism' [x 457] is analogous not only to Charles I's absolutism but also to the rule of Cromwell's Major-Generals, regarded by radicals as 'Turkish bashaws': revolutionaries who, once in power, become totalitarians. Satan thus represents problems relevant to Milton's own cause, for 'the problem of liberty turned out to be insoluble in the sort of [bourgeois] revolution' that Milton experienced [366]. In so far as *Paradise Lost* suggests a solution, it is the doctrine of perfectibility, in which ultimately all things return to the 'all in all' of God. On this Hill comments that 'the ultimate ideal state is not monarchical, because the concepts of power . . . have no meaning when we are all gods'. In this millenarian expectation Milton's position is analogous to the Marxist idea of the state's eventual redundancy in a classless society [303–4]. Certainly there is a suggestive correlation between Marxist and Christian notions of historical teleology, and Marxist critics in particular tend to emphasise Milton's millenarianism. But perfectibility in Milton is not quite a matter of becoming 'gods' – that echoes Satan's temptation of Eve [IX 710–17] – rather, of becoming 'one *with* God'. 'For regal sceptre then no more shall need; / God shall be all in all' [III 340–1]. Nevertheless, Hill's vigorous reassertion of a radical Milton was a very welcome riposte to those who had toned him down.

According to Milner [1979], however, Hill was insufficiently rigorous in both Marxist and literary-critical terms. Finding Hill's historical method 'surprisingly depoliticised' [198],

Milner argues persuasively that Milton's ideology was consistent in terms of revolutionary independency, so that far from sharing some radical Leveller views, as Hill contends, Milton was antagonistic to them [200]. His ideology is the classic bourgeois revolutionary's, which destroys one political hierarchy only to replace it with a more congenial class dominance. As *Paradise Lost*'s hierarchical Heaven and Hell show, this alternative system is meritocracy, epitomised in the elevation of the Son [III 309–11; Milner, 95–136, 155]. Milton's attitudes are analogous to Marxist revolutionary notions of hierarchy, and his central concern with the rule of reason over passion in man – *Paradise Lost* showing that 'ultimately *history* will secure the triumph of reason' – approximates to the Marxist historical teleology [156, 166]. However, in contending that the epic reflects Milton's rationalist system of thought, in which the concept of God is effectively 'irrelevant' to man's ability to progress, Milner finds that the biblical myth 'runs counter' to Milton's real theme [VIII 635–7; Milner, 155–9]. The 'notion of divine determinism' collides with Milton's deepest convictions about the rationalistic voluntarism of human free will [154]. In this argument Milner comes curiously close to the classic humanist position on Milton, and indeed cites approvingly Willey's notion that the Fall shows a humanistic contradiction in Milton's theology [158]. To see Milton's God as irrelevant to his thought seems (at least) quixotic.

Opposing Marxist notions of Milton's ideological ambivalence, Davies [1984] contends that *Paradise Lost*'s conception of kingship is not monothetic. Not only is there is no necessary correspondence between divine and human regality, but monarchical images vary according to their context. Satanic is compared with Asiatic despotism (reflecting the contemporary European terror of Turkish aggression and the Muslim threat to Christianity) and to Roman imperialism, whereas God's monarchy is a celestially improved form of paternal feudalism. Satan betrays the liege-lord whom he should love. Davies's argument broadly supports the generally accepted view that, as Milton had argued in *Eikonoklastes*, earthly kings were sacrilegious to claim over others an authority similar to God's. Satan's desire to rule, in Heaven, Hell, or earth, implies that monarchical power is really rebellion against the sole true authority [IV 957–61; Lewis, 73–80].

Evidently, the Kingdom in Milton's politics has as much to do with soldiering as with ruling. If the War in Heaven is orchestrated by God to prove his omnipotence in the person of the Son [Revard, 1980, 129–97; Fallon, 1984, 228; VI 880], equally Christ in his chariot is the apocalyptic Messiah, at once victorious warrior and king. Revard acknowledges that Christ is a warrior, but remains wedded to the antimilitaristic notion of Milton, insisting that Christ is not imitable in mortal militarism. Instead, armed with gunpowder, Satan in his conspiracy represents a political threat for Milton's own time, when the Gunpowder Plot was remembered as an instance of the way in which his plotting manifests itself in human affairs [88–92, 107]. Satan is the archetype of all malign political subversion. In the War in Heaven as in Parliamentarian sermons, however, it is suggested that 'faith may attain primacy over force' [122]. This antimilitarism is contested by Fallon [1983], who stresses that Milton was not merely familiar with military manuals [Freeman, 1981], but had observed London's trained bands at drill as well as experiencing the Civil War's military vicissitudes at close hand. Given Milton's support for the New Model Army, Fallon thinks it illogical to see *Paradise Lost* as antimilitaristic, even though Satan's heroic characteristics are undermined. Presented as an effective general rallying his troops in I, he is warned off combat with Death [II], flies from Gabriel [IV], and when finally brought to blows is wounded by Michael [VI]. In x he flees 'terrified' from the Son. Both his apparent stature and his actual degeneration are presented, then, 'in military terms' [174–9]. But so is God's omnipotence. In the War in Heaven is crystallised Milton's conception of God as 'glory', presented in military and political forms. Equally, Satan's defeat is a matter of tactical failure reflecting his spiritual error [222–32]. Demonstrating Milton's familiarity with military history, the War symbolises in effect 'a vivid lesson in the nature of evil' precisely because evil and loyal angels appear so alike, but are so different [235]. Equally, Satan the specious politician reflects Milton's experience of corrupt revolutionaries who distort the true cause [173]. In this respect Fallon subscribes to criticism's recent emphases, which have tended to deny that Satan can be simply paralleled with

either Cromwell or Charles I and II. Most are now agreed that
Satan's rebellion is effectively tyrannous rather than
libertarian: dividing rather between those who find this an
understandable paradox and those who regard it as a
fundamental contradiction in 'Christian Liberty'.

Psychology and myth

If Milton's revolutionary attitudes have presented problems,
equally the religious theme of *Paradise Lost* has been off-putting
to many non-Christian readers. Assuming that nowadays few
readers are theists, critics of the 1950s and 60s in particular
favoured the notion that this poem is still generally accessible
as a 'mythic' formulation of reality – myth possessing a power
over our minds which is quite independent of belief. Meditating
upon Milton's presentation of the Fall as a psychological
paradox (Adam's understandable human love for Eve is
equally a 'fond' or foolish uxoriousness), Bergonzi thought that
'One does not need to be a believing Christian to feel the force of
this' representation of contradictions frequently experienced in
human life [1960, 179]. Kermode goes further: if we confuse
Paradise Lost with the Bible we will miss its force as a myth of the
'primitive' tragedy of Death. For the same reason we will ignore
Milton's counter-emphasis, in Paradise, upon a life-affirming
celebration of sensuality [1960, 102–5]. Here Kermode gives a
mythic, 'Dionysiac' reading of Milton's much-noted
materialism, which makes his angels eat and digest, and impels
his eloquent assertion that – 'whatever hypocrites' say [IV 744]
– there was sex in the unfallen Paradise.
    Although mythological criticism was first applied to *Paradise
Lost* by Bodkin [1934], in its recent guise it has been most
influenced by Frye [1957], who attempted to establish a
systematic approach to literary criticism, based upon a
'scientific' taxonomy of archetypes. Deriving from Jung's
theory of the collective unconscious, or 'race memory' which
surfaces in our dreams, archetypes are universal images which
recur in myth and ritual because they correspond to
unchanging elements in the unconscious. Reflecting these,
literature represents the 'total dream' of mankind. Equally, by
triggering memory of archetypes, literature speaks with

peculiar force to basic human desires. In this light literature is dignified as an essential constituent of human culture. However, Frye's critical system is susceptible to critique from several angles [see e.g. Hartman, 1970, 24–41; Lentricchia, 1980, 2–26]. Although Frye is attempting to get beyond the New Criticism ('close reading') of the 1950s, he shares with the New Critics a neglect of the historical context and political ideologies of texts. For him all texts exist in a realm of universal and timeless archetypes. Archetypal taxonomy also blurs the distinctions between texts. Are texts 'good' simply because – whether by Milton or a pulp novelist – they contain archetypes? Do these archetypes automatically trigger the reader's response, simply by virtue of being there, rather than because they are in a *literary* work? What happens if, as Waldock objected to Bodkin's reading of *Paradise Lost* [1947, 129–35], an archetype fails to work on the reader because its literary presentation is unsuccessful?

Frye is sufficiently subtle to avoid this problem in his most influential essay on the poem [1969], where he focuses on its overt use of dreams and their reflection of an archetypal paradisal state for humanity. Adam experiences two dreams, the first of Eden's fruit trees, the second of Eve. Both are evoked by appetites, for food and sex. In contrast, Eve's demonically-inspired dream, in its 'orgasmic rhythm', manifests recognisably Freudian symbolism of sexual 'flying'. In this respect her dream anticipates postlapsarian consciousness (Freud equals fallen), the degeneration of these appetites into greed and lust. Similarly, Satan, who inspires the dream, represents fallen appetites taken to the demonic level, as 'force and fraud', here exerted in a symbolically sexual seduction [24]. The fallen character of dreams as wish-fulfilment represents our distance from the paradisal state, in which human appetites were effortlessly matched with their capacity to be satisfied. Dreams supply the satisfactions we can no longer gratify in reality. In this account Frye reveals that utopian metaphysical urge which, Lentricchia claims, finds its own wish-fulfilment in literary freedom from ugly historical reality. Frye's method does, however, allow him to highlight Milton's spiritualised pointing of dreams. When, after the Fall, Adam receives instruction from Michael there is a significant change from the paradisal situation of Raphael's instruction [v–viii]. Since the fallen Adam can no longer be relied upon to relay enlightenment to Eve – something she had trusted in then – now she receives her own distinctive revelation of God's plan, in a dream [19; xi 369]. The implication, although Frye does not press it, is that dreams remain our mode of access to the primitive natural world – so to say, the divine world – from which we are now alienated. In this crucial divorce of humanity from environment the sexual division 'represent[s] the polarizing of man's existence between God and Nature, creation and creature' [21]. In *Paradise Lost* appear the archetypal images of that polarisation, manifested as the male and female 'principles' in the natural order. Adam's relationship to Eve thus replicates the male principle of the wind ['Zephyr', v 16] affecting the female principle of the flowers. Such images are related to the traditional characterisation – as in the Song of Songs – of the female body as an enclosed garden [23–4]. As Frye notes that Adam's aubade to Eve is drawn from the Song, we may infer that this echo represents Adam's authority over her as analogous to that of God over him, a 'male principle'. Such archetypes are not only basic to Milton's presentation of the Christian truth he sees 'blurred' in classical myths, but exist at the very psychic level at which poetic imagination operates [26–7]. At this level too the reader responds to the myth. While we are not told the precise content of Eve's dream – only that she is assured of Christ's victory – we can nevertheless 'recognise' its nature: 'far below [this epic's] rarefied pinnacle of rational vision, there lies a humiliated mother dreaming of the vengeance of her mighty son' [47].

Frye thinks that Milton's Eve reflects a crucial ambivalence in myths of the Mother-Goddess, fertile and protective yet frequently a deceiver and destroyer too. Hebraic myth suggests an alter-ego for Eve, the dangerous Lilith. Influenced by Frye, the anthropology of Eliade and Jung's psychology, Duncan [1980] extends this investigation of Eve's simultaneous figuration as the sacred Mary and a wanton Venus. The Garden represents her 'fruitful womb', compared to that of 'Mary, second Eve', who brings forth the redeemer of Eve's children [v 385–9]. In a Jungian light Paradise itself is symbolic of 'the Mother' and hence of fertility and redemption. The redemptive Virgin signifies an advanced stage in the development of the anima, or feminine element of consciousness, a stage reached by Eve only after the Fall [48–9]. This is because, for Jung, the Christian Eden symbolises selfhood, the coming to self-consciousness: and this process actually requires that transition from childhood to consciousness which occurs at the Tree of Knowledge. So this process of 'individuation' is itself 'the Fortunate Fall' which Milton describes [37–42]. Eve's fascination for Adam [v 95] is precisely that she embodies the anima in his own nature, by means of which his consciousness develops. Equally, in her dream Satan implants animus in Eve, which emerges as her truculence against Adam [ix 205–374]. Linked to the processes of developing consciousness is the child's attitude to the Mother. Initially the paradisal womb, she becomes 'terrible' when fear of incest supervenes. This stage is, in *Paradise Lost*, the advent of sin – Sin herself, an incestuous mother, entering Paradise [x 602, 585–9] and transforming its image of maternity. As a whole, this poem 'provides one of the best examples of Frye's super-myth . . . of the search for identity' [44].

While Duncan's anthropological background is so detailed as to risk our losing sight of the poem altogether, MacCaffrey's [1959] is so exclusively concerned with the epic's 'myth' as to verge on myopia. She subordinates narrative to imagery, arguing that Milton's own 'mythical narrative slights chronology' [45]. It does begin in the middle, retracking on Satan's rebellion and the Creation in v–vii. For MacCaffrey the relevant structure is that of myth itself, which works by 'images, not ideas' [5]. Structure evolves from images of movement, especially from an 'inverted v' pattern established by the poem's drop into Hell, followed by ascent into Heaven and descent to earth [iii–iv]: a 'spatial' perspective on the poem which is further developed by Cope [1962]. Weber [1976] complains that MacCaffrey and Cope suggest a structure of meaning in the poem which 'is held together only by the critic's metaphor', and breaks down when the text is examined [82–6]. Citing especially Burden's defence of the narrative [1967], Weber notes that the fact that Milton's narrative is non-chronological does not make it any less a narrative [86–7]. But in MacCaffrey's scheme, the details of a particular story would get in the way of her assumption that essentially there is only

one pattern common to all myths, and that prototype is
reflected in *Paradise Lost* too. This is the mythic rite of passage, a
separation followed by initiation and return [17–23]. Here this
quest pattern is represented first by Satan, cast out of Heaven,
voyaging through Chaos in order to reach Paradise. Other
wanderings in the poem anticipate or echo his journey. All
replicate the basic human experience of struggling through
darkness to light, the imagery of light in fact pervading the
poem [191]. Mythic pattern exemplifies the Christian
pilgrimage to salvation and return, that 'Light after light well
used they shall attain, / And to the end persisting, safe arrive'
[III, 194–7; 205]. The myth of life as a 'wandering' merges with
Milton's ethic of the wayfaring Christian, showing fallen man
exiled in history, an exile most potently imaged in the final lines
of the poem [191]. At this point the theme is transferred from
Satan, 'the archetypal exile', to mankind – to us [179]. The
point of meeting between the two journeys, demonic and
human, has already been signified in III 633, 'His journeys end
and our beginning woe' [205]. Contesting this notion of spatial
repetition, Weber thinks it 'misrepresents the poem's emotive
effects'. In MacCaffrey's view upward movement in space,
towards light, 'should image virtue', but in Satan's journey this
is evidently not the case [82].

Certainly MacCaffrey's elevation of Satan as a human
archetype raises more strongly the very question it is designed
to answer: whether an attractive Satan undermines the poem's
theology. If, as Werblowsky [1980] suggests, Satan shares the
mythic value of Prometheus, Milton is certainly playing with
fire. Prometheus the fire-bringer was also light-bearer (cf.
'Lucifer', Satan's angelic name), whose revolt against the
prohibitions of Zeus may have transgressed divine law but was
absolutely necessary to man's survival. The likeness of Satan to
the Promethean archetype is clearest in their similar refusal to
bow the knee to deity [I 111–16] and their own proximity to the
divine plane of existence [132–5]. Theologically, of course,
Milton portrays Satan's rebellion as an unnecessary
perversion, but the Prometheus myth shows that the same
impulse is vital to man's evolution, hubris being a condition of
his attaining conscious being. Satan represents this primitive
process which nevertheless kindles 'Life in its specifically
human sense' [136–7]. The price of this development is guilt for

transgression, and that loneliness of selfhood which is archetypally correspondent to birth-trauma, severance from the mother. In *Paradise Lost* this guilt is represented in Christian terms, so that Milton tries to transfer the positive charge of the Promethean image to Christ, another life-bringer. However, his more successful portrayal of Satan the 'anti-god' means that the 'Greek in Milton got the upper hand over the Hebrew', says Werblowsky [145–6], reanimating the old humanist version of Milton.

However, the notion that birth-trauma is a fundamental archetype in *Paradise Lost* translates humanist readings into a different dimension. On the one hand, Rosenblatt [1972] sees the influence of the biblical Exodus on Milton's War in Heaven, Shawcross [1982] suggests that the epic as a whole reflects the archetype of exodus or exile, and Martz [1980] that this is the 'epic of exile'. On the other, we have Werblowsky's and MacCaffrey's lonely humanity, expelled from the Paradisal Womb. With prescience, Bergonzi remarked in 1960 that the poem's meaning 'might well have a good deal to do with . . . "the birth trauma" ' [180]. More generally, 'Milton was early seized with the Freudian insight that the only paradises are those we have lost' [LeComte, 1984, 198]. The lost sexual paradise of Adam and Eve's prelapsarian marriage is pointedly contrasted by Rudat with the post-coital exhaustion brought on by lapsarian coupling [1982, 110; ix 1042–5]. Adapting Augustine in a Freudian manner, Milton's personal version of the history of human sexuality provides the rationale for the Fall and implies Milton's spiritual argument. Seduced by the serpent's 'phallic dance' [ix 501–2], Eve is motivated by penis-envy to eat the apple, in the conviction that it will impart to her Adam's phallicness. However, intrinsically the apple symbolises the vagina, so that Eve becomes sexually self-aware, self-seduced. Paradoxically she has acquired not Adam's superiority but his 'sexual excitability', thus rendering herself dependent upon him for its satisfaction. In Adam's case, involuntary sexual arousal is consequent upon the Fall – his initial reaction to the apple is an erection [ix 1011–13] – and this involuntariness represents his loss of superiority, of control. In a similar way the phallic serpent is punished by losing his erect stance. Like Eve, although Adam has succumbed to (vagina) envy, he loses more than he gains, for in

surrendering to her power over him 'Adam emasculates himself'
by eating the female fruit. Now Eve controls his sexuality
[112–15]. For this sexual process of spiritual Fall the trigger
was Eve's erection-dream, of which the serpent's dance
subconsciously reminds her [118]. In this reading the Fall is,
precisely, the emergence of Freudian sexuality.

In the emergence of poets there is also, according to Bloom
[1973], a literary process equivalent to the Freudian 'family
romance'. Strong poetic precursors are (as it were) fathers
whose successors experience an 'anxiety of influence' – a poetic
Oedipus Complex. In this respect the pre-eminence of Milton
amongst English poets rendered him, especially when his
influence was at its apogee in the eighteenth century, a
particularly testing 'father'. For Bloom he is the 'great
Inhibitor'. To prevent his influence smothering their own
work, strong poets have to revolt against this Father-God much
as Milton's Satan did. By deliberately and creatively
'misreading' the precursor's poems – as Blake did Milton's –
they find their own voices, overcoming this poetic crisis of
identity. (Bloom's theory is critically examined by Lentricchia,
his reassertion of Milton's malign influence contested by
Griffin [1986].) According to Kerrigan [1983], however,
Milton the poet was himself crucially affected by the Oedipus
Complex. His tardiness in writing his *magnum opus* [cf.
LeComte, 1973; Tayler, 1979] was not adventitious but a
psychological necessity. Only once he had overcome the
oedipal problem could he sublimate it in the epic's relations
between God, Son, and Satan. Kerrigan's brilliant study does
not simply render Milton's religion into psychiatric terms, but
shows what might have been his psychology of belief. One way
or another, the fertile field of psychoanalytic studies seems to
suggest that Milton had read Freud after all!

Reader and text

What used to be the major critical question – whether Satan
was so compelling as to disrupt the 'official' narrative of
Paradise Lost – obviously involved assumptions about a clash
between Milton's intention and the reader's actual response to
the poem. Fish [1967] was the first to try to reconcile intention

and response primarily in terms of a theory about how the reader's response develops in the course of the poem. (Later [1980] he would postulate a general theory of reader-response which, like so many other literary theories, had whetted its teeth on *Paradise Lost*.) In his view, Milton actually intends that we should misread his poem. When the reader is seduced by Satan's rhetoric, s/he is placed in a position similar to that of Eve seduced by the serpent's [261]. Whenever Milton's own voice intervenes to correct our response, he is deliberately disappointing our expectations in order to show that we too are corrupted – fallen readers. By constantly misleading and correcting our reading of the action, Milton makes us 'angry at the epic voice . . . for being right, for insisting that we become our own critics' [9]. In this way we are gradually rendered suspicious of our own reactions, becoming, like Adam, 'not deceived' about our own sinfulness. The reader does not observe a dramatic presentation of the action, but rather participates in it: 'The poem's centre of reference is its reader', her/himself experiencing the Fall [1, 11–12]. Contradicting Waldock's Satanist reading, Fish examines that moment in Book I when Satan makes an impressive speech of defiance [I 84–124]. Waldock opined that Milton, worried about this impressiveness, hastily compensates with the clumsily didactic comment that Satan is merely 'Vaunting aloud, but racked with deep despair' [I 126; 1947, 77–8]. However, according to Fish the blatancy of Milton's rebuke is precisely what shocks the reader into re-examining her/his initial response to the speech [4–9]. Fish's ingenious inversion of Waldock's argument – turning Milton's alleged clumsiness into a deliberate and successful strategy for manipulating the reader – was precisely Fish's mistake, according to Weber [1976, 89–95]. For Fish reads Milton 'through' the Satanist critics. It is impossible, Weber says, to construe 'Vaunting aloud. . .' as a direct rebuke to the reader unless one has first read Waldock's paraphrase of it.

Weber also attacks Fish's contention that the poem is constantly presenting the reader with 'choices between black-and-white alternatives' of interpretation. Fish had suggested that when the newly-created Eve looks into the pool [IV 453–67], the allusion to Narcissus may be taken in two ways. Either it suggests Eve's vanity, and hints at her capacity to Fall,

or it could simply refer to her childlike innocence. It all depends
how far the comparison to Narcissus is meant to reach, whether
it includes his self-induced demise. Is Eve different from
Narcissus in that she will not suffer his fate? She does, after all,
consent to abandon her own reflection when Adam and God
instruct that she should. According to Fish, however, the
reader 'cannot possibly . . . ignore the problem' of whether the
allusion hints at Eve's sinful propensities, a problem raised
again by her dream [216–19]. But Weber suggests that we can
read the Narcissus allusion in the 'wrong' way (wrong in Fish's
scheme) and still come up with the 'right' answer – that Eve,
like Adam, is not inherently weak to temptation, but simply
'capable of error', an error here corrected. In any case, Weber
insists, we are not faced with an 'interpretive choice' here but
rather asked to analyse all the various implications of the
incident, including its parallel to the new-created Adam's own
awakening. He too first displays a fascination with his own
appearance. For Fish the reader's alternative choices tend to
reflect a choice 'between the affirmation and the doubt of God',
but Weber cannot see this as a direct consequence of how we
understand the Narcissus allusion. However, such a
consequence is possible if we think a Narcissan Eve implies that
God made her faulty, and thus as it were caused her to fall. This
would suggest Empson's cruel God, punishing humankind for
what he made them do. Yet, Weber says, Eve's capacity for sin,
like Adam's, merely shows that she is 'free to fall' and therefore
that God truly allowed his creatures free will. She makes her
own decision to stop being a Narcissus and become Adam's
wife. This narrative occurrence provides a context for the
allusion, which is not interpretable in isolation from it [92].
The implication is that, in his anxiety to follow the moment-by-
moment effects of the poem's language upon the reader, Fish
loses sight of the dramatic plot. As we saw, Fish does indeed
wish to transfer the drama of *Paradise Lost* from the narrative to
the reader's consciousness. One of the strengths of this view is
its reflection of Milton's stated intention, which is to justify
God's way '*to men*' – to his readers. Fish, like Rajan [1947], is
thinking of a seventeenth-century reader's reactions, but
Crosman tries to extend this kind of approach to modern
readers too. Thinking less in terms of interpretive choices and
more in terms of ambivalent responses, Crosman suggests that

Milton's portrait of the serpent as a pompous orator in the
Temptation scene [IX 664–78] adds a comic dimension which
co-exists with our tragic sense of Eve's predicament. That
comic element makes the Fall seem less inevitable (the serpent
less powerful), thus confirming Eve's free will [1980, 174–5].
Inherent in such a 'modern' extension of the reader's response
is the possibility that because modern it need not, after all, bear
any relation to Milton's own intentions. Wheeler [1974] seems
to be trying to avoid such a complete disconnection when he
insists that the reader's freedom to interpret the text 'in modern
terms' would have been approved by Milton 'because of his
own commitment to liberty' [1974, 16–17].

Certainly Fish's notion that Milton 'harasses' his readers has
evoked complaint that Milton must have expected them to be
masochists [Samuel, 211]. More common is an emphasis upon
Milton's attempt to 'accommodate' his readers. The
traditional idea of accommodation addressed the problem of
how the supernatural realm may be portrayed in terms that
human beings can understand. Raphael describes the problem
when telling Adam the story of the War in Heaven: 'how shall I
relate to human sense the invisible exploits of warring
spirits. . .?' The answer is the anthropomorphic method –
'what surmounts the reach of human sense I shall
delineate . . ./ By likening spiritual to corporeal forms' [V
564–73]. Since Milton had a materialist view of divine forms
anyway – something reflected in Raphael's statement that
earth and heaven are possibily more alike than is usually
thought [574–6] – this anthropomorphic method forges close
links between the transcendent and earthly planes of existence
in *Paradise Lost* [Ryken, 1970]. In the angelic instructions by
Raphael and Michael, Lewalski thinks, Milton shows the
angels using literary genres to accommodate their narrations to
the minds of their human auditors [1983]. We, too, recognise
the genres and hence how we should respond to them.

   In this suggestion Lewalski is evoking the 'ideal reader', one
scholarly enough to recognise the literary traditions which
Milton utilises and thereby understand his meaning. For
deconstructionist critics that 'ideal reader' is a chimaera: a text
has as many meanings as it has readers, there is no 'ideal' or
actual single meaning to which the text can be reduced.
Derrida, the foremost deconstructive theorist, attributes

traditional critics' desire to discover the 'ultimate' meaning of a text to the 'logocentric' tradition of Western thought. In this tradition it is believed that words refer to the world beyond them, that they have meaning. In the Derridean view words are not only disjunct from 'reality', but in the very process of expressing meaning they signify its absence. (That is, there is no secure relationship between the semantic sign and what it purports to signify.) Language only gives the illusion of something beyond itself, an illusion that is constantly breaking down. To posit meaning – as opposed, that is, to the reader's own construction of meaning out of the text s/he reads – is to be logocentric: word-worshipping, in a sense. That impulse to assign meaning is closely related to a belief in the 'meaning' of the world. The Christian or logocentric tradition (in scripture Christ is The Word, the logos) ascribes a metaphysical meaning to the universe, a 'presence' or absolute state of being. In the deconstructive view there is only 'absence' – deprivation of meaning, illusory being, a God who is not there. Philosophically, deconstruction is an outgrowth of the sceptical stream of thought in which Nietzsche and Freud figure so largely. In literary terms, deconstruction seeks to demonstrate how the text's claim to establish meaning necessarily breaks down. Given the anti-theological implications of this theory, *Paradise Lost's* religious claims and its status as a 'canonical' text necessarily pose an exciting challenge to deconstructionist method. That challenge can be stated as the question, 'Is it possible to read a theological epic anti-theologically?'

Yes. Bouchard [1974] says that since Milton was an iconoclast (as *Eikonoklastes* testifies), this anti-didacticism informs his atheistic poem. The idol-worshipper here is Satan, whose method is to enslave his followers by didactic exhortation, 'foster[ing] belief in the image' [68]: a method most clearly seen in the fallen Eve, who worships the Tree as an idol of magical power and knowledge [ix 795–810]. Milton, on the contrary, knows that the search for truth, for certainty, is always doomed to disappointment. But human liberty lies precisely in the fact that free will allows mankind so to search. Far from preventing this, or demanding worship of himself as an absolute authority, Milton's God is the first image-breaker. The death of his Son, who is his own image, represents his erasure of himself. Because God (authority, origin, the worshipped) is dead, man is free [63–4]. In other words, Milton's attachment to the theme of free will shows the epic's atheist tendency. Although Johnson complained that Milton saw the world 'through the spectacles of books', in a deconstructionist view this is what human beings habitually do anyway. So Milton's epic does not claim to represent 'reality', being concerned rather with 'the nature of the sign' [10]. In interpretation we search for meaning, a search Adams learns at the end to give up, and to live by faith instead [98]. This is one of the reasons why we should not read the epic sequentially, from beginning to end, but 'from both ends'. For sequence implies progress towards a conclusion, and that assumes a 'determinacy' of meaning – that interpretation has an end. Rather, the end of the poem is also the beginning, both focusing on 'the solitariness of the speaker' [113]. This is, of course, the irredeemable loneliness of the human 'subject' or individual in a Nietzschean universe. That perspective affects Adam and Eve's portrayal too. Far from being splendid perfect beings in the prelapsarian books (as Lewis had contended), they are bunglers: an accurate and unflattering 'reflection of the reader' [65–6].

This raises a problem, though. Bouchard has insisted that *Paradise Lost* is not didactic because mimetic (viz. not imitating 'reality'). But can this notion hold if Adam and Eve are as it were mimetic of the reader? It should be said, however, that Bouchard only comes up against such problems because he is trying to remain attentive to Milton despite the anti-authorial tendency of deconstruction. So Bouchard is deeply engaged with the text, whereas Rapaport [1983] seems unwilling to get too near it. He wants to demonstrate that Milton's inconsistent ideology anticipates the deconstructive recognition of indeterminacy, the instability of 'meaning'. In explicating the indeterminacy of Eve (her ambivalent signification of the Mother-Goddess and the Destroyer or transgressor), he places her characterisation as a 'flower' within the context of Derrida's reading of a novel by Genet. In Genet a thief is a flower: so is Eve the flower who steals the apple. Writers are thieves too, in that writing transgresses or usurps 'voice' (by which is meant, in part, speech: writing as it were pretends to be speech). In this sense the 'sign' of Eve implicates the writer Milton, too, whose iconoclasm is a transgression [12–15]. Eve's undecidability shows that her fall is undecidability too, and is indeed the condition of writing [59–73]. Actually, according to Rapaport, there is 'no' Fall in this text. While Kendrick [1986] thinks (oddly enough!) that there *is* a Fall, like the 'humanist' critics he sees a fundamental contradiction in Milton's presentation of it. *Paradise Lost* is constituted of contradictions between epic and hexameron, genres which reflect respectively freedom (an 'ethic of permission') and theological predestination (the official 'ethic of prohibition' against the eating of the apple). In Marxist-poststructuralist terms, this contradiction shows the problems of seventeenth-century culture, when the notion of an ethical 'subject' (or individual) is emerging under capitalism.

Both Rapaport [32] and Bouchard see Satan in Freudian terms, as an example of 'repetition compulsion' in his 'doomed imitation of God' [68]. Hartman [1965] suggests that in the opening books Satan's portrayal is not as strong as the Satanists thought, because Milton's poem includes a 'counterplot' which constantly runs alongside the apparent narrative. Particularly in his similes, Milton suggests an alternative view of Hell's scene: the serene plot of God's providence, under which the demonic characters unwittingly act. In the famous 'Vallombrosa' simile [I 302–11] the lifelessness of the leaves, to which the fallen angels are compared, places an implicit but ironic perspective on Satan's attempt to rouse them up off the lake of fire. Here an allusion to the defeated and scattered 'Memphian' army imagistically suggests God's power to scatter the fallen angels, as he has done before. So the ' "plot counterplot" [shows that] the hand of Satan is not ultimately distinguishable from the will of God' [391–2]. Hell's supposed power to disturb the Creation is always affected by this distancing of the reader from Hell's activities. Hell is never allowed to seem 'secure' [389]. The counterplot we experience in reading *Paradise Lost* is an indeterminacy, in effect, a sliding of meanings which reflects the difficulty of the ethical life when we possess free will, an ability and responsibility to make choices.

For Parker [1979] this indeterminacy is extended by various 'suspensions' in the narrative of the poem. Yet narrative itself, according to Nyquist, is not homogeneous throughout the epic. In IV–VIII there is much use of retrospective narration – by

Raphael, Eve, and Adam – which interrupts the fluency of plot. The paradisal location is matched by a mode of discourse which creates 'a dilatory space where meaning itself is to some degree suspended' in an arrested 'fictional present' [1984, 199–200]. Even the dialogue given to Eve and Adam is undynamic, has a ritual ceremonial quality [203–5]. In contrast to this suspension which conveys innocence and tranquillity is Satan's scheme, which rolls forward towards its goal of destruction. Before the Fall, however, Eve and Adam are locked in stasis (despite those critics who contend that they develop in action). So Eve's dream, for instance, cannot be read as the origin of her fall, for such cause-and-effect continuity is contradicted by the way this episode is locked into the past by retrospective narration. We are only told of the dream [v 28–93] after Satan's presence in Eden has been discovered by the sentinel angels, and this placing prevents our regarding the dream as dangerous. Displaced from sequential narrative, the dream episode 'is virtually self-deconstructing' [201–2]. Conversely, after Milton announces the tragic mood in which the Fall will be described [ix 5–6], the epic's action is related in direct, fluent narrative, and dialogue between Eve and Adam becomes interactively dialectical. Before, they simply addressed each other: now they respond to each other in a psychological process. In the Separation Scene [ix 205–384] this verisimilitude invites the reader to identify with their experience, and prepares for the psychological exchange in the Temptation scene [ix 531–781]. When Adam and Eve later quarrel in assigning blame, they recall, and interpret, the Separation dialogue in a fallen way. The reader, knowing they are corrupt before they realise it themselves, sees that the 'text' of the Separation Scene is 'now being displaced by its readings' [227]. If, like Eve and Adam, we were to read into the Separation the Fall's causation, we would be succumbing to the same delusions. Paradise was not 'determined' by such consequential action, and that was the essence of the paradisal state. It is not character flaw, but mode of narrative, which signifies the movement to a fallen consciousness. As Nyquist's reading shows, deconstructive criticism is at its best when analysing the postlapsarian effects in this poem, which are so congruent with the lonely Freudian subject in modern thought.

Feminist approaches

Feminist criticism has been the most fecund recent growth area in Milton studies, but the general issue of Milton's attitude towards women has been standard critical equipment for some time. Arguably 'the one thing that almost every undergraduate "knows" about Milton is that he was a misogynist' [Rudrum, 1969, 13]. But things are not as simple as the popular view suggests. One of the first avowedly feminist critics of Milton insists that 'It is unreasonable to argue that Milton was a misogynist' [Landy, 1976, 11]. If so, how did that view gain such hold? Its most significant source is biographical, the failure of Milton's first marriage to Marie Powell, commonly assumed to be the motive for his tracts arguing the legitimacy of divorce. Even in his own lifetime, political opponents cast that marriage in his face, along with anything else that could defame him. But the decisive popularisation of Milton's misogyny was Johnson's. After a caustic account of Marie's desertion and its blow to Milton's arrogant self-esteem, Johnson remarks that Milton's enthusiasm for liberty did not extend to his own household. Here 'he was severe and arbitrary', and his writings display 'a Turkish contempt of females as subordinate and inferior beings . . . He thought woman made only for obedience, and man only for rebellion' [91]. In *Paradise Lost*, Johnson noted, there was constant stress upon the superiority of Adam to Eve [101]. When T. S. Eliot raised a storm against Milton this charge was superadded to the literary debunking of *Paradise Lost* – most spectacularly by Robert Graves's satirical novel on Milton's marriage [1942]. In the same atmosphere, Tillyard saw in Adam's misogynist vituperations after the Fall Milton's own expression of resentment against Marie [1930, 265].

Yet the reading of biography into the poem is challengable not only by theoretical arguments about the externality of author to text, but also by a context in which biography itself is implicated. Milton's Puritanism allied him with Reformation attitudes towards women and marriage, which rejected the Roman Catholic preference for celibacy and derogation of sex, even within marriage, unless strictly subordinate to the procreative motive. In the divorce tracts, Milton himself eloquently argued that the primary end of marriage was not procreation but companionship, or 'mutual conversation' (i.e. all forms of interpersonal exchange). In making compatibility primary, Milton was avant-garde even among reformers [Halkett, 1970], who had generally sought to identify women's status in marriage beyond their traditionally designated role as 'sexual vessels'. The reformist enthusiasm for godly marriage, as a state encompassing both physical and spiritual fulfilment, is reflected in Milton's hymn to 'wedded love' [iv 750–75; Haller, 1969]. *Paradise Lost* is unique amongst epics in its domestic focus, and 'Marriage is the crucial issue in the fall of Adam' [Burden, 150; Toliver, 1976]. In the light of religious tradition too, Eve's role is unusually sizeable, and Milton's insistence that Eve and Adam enjoyed intercourse *before* the Fall verges on the heterodox. It can even be argued that in his Eden sex is portrayed as the height of paradisal bliss, a level of joy irrecoverable in postlapsarian intercourse [Lindenbaum, 1974]. Sex is further dignified by Raphael's information that even angels experience such union. Generally the epic implies a sort of sexual cosmology in which Eve and Adam's union participates: 'two great sexes animate the world' [viii 151]. Milton's doctrine of perfectibility entails the ultimate reunion of all things with God, so that human elevation towards the divine state can be understood in terms of the neo-Platonic ascent from earthly to heavenly love [Boyette, 1967]. Given the high profile Milton grants to sex, and the narrator's provocative emphasis upon it, the poem has an obvious relation to modern sexual politics. These have been examined from various angles, feminist criticism being a house of many mansions in which various literary theories are directed towards issues of gender.

Such issues are sometimes implicitly raised by male critics' remarks, as for instance when Lindenbaum suggests that Milton is 'defining man' by 'our response to Eve's beauty' [1974, 300]. Where exactly does this leave the heterosexual female reader? In a 'feminist' essay Aers and Hodge conclude that in the postlapsarian coupling 'Eve is *active* now as she never was in paradisal sexuality' [1981, 149–50]. Apparently they have not noticed that to Adam Eve is now a sexual object rather than a person. They complain of Adam's 'superior love' before the Fall [iv 492–502], but not of his statement after the Fall that Eve is a plaything that he proposes to 'enjoy' [xi 1027–32].

They often have recourse to invoking their 'female students', but many feminists would argue that no male reader can vicariously speak for his female counterpart. For her two moments in particular provoke revulsion: Milton's insistence that Eve and Adam are 'Not equal', and that Adam is the image of God with direct access to the deity, 'He for God only, she for God in him' [IV 296–9]. If, as is commonly thought, *Paradise Lost* evokes a cosmic system of hierarchies, Milton here emphasises Eve's subordination to Adam as analogous to his relationship with God. The implications of this view depend on what Eve and Adam represent, a matter of puzzlement to Tillyard [1930, 258]. If, as many feminists do, we take it that their relationship is a prototype and prescription for sexual relations generally – and Milton's sanctification of marriage seems to follow this orthodox thinking – then he is justifying the authority of men over women, the 'inferior' sex. It can be said that Milton has no choice but to follow the misogynistic narrative of his source, Genesis, but according to Rogers [1966, 151–9], of the two extant versions of Genesis Milton deliberately chose the more misogynistic Jahvist's version. That choice reflects Milton's ambivalence about women: highly responsive to them, as LeComte also has shown [1978], yet fearful of their power to degrade men by seduction. Because this power must be controlled, Eve is portrayed as subordinate, constantly deferring to Adam's sway [IV 295–308, 635–8]. Ultimately, despite Milton's unusually strong proponence of marriage and hence of women's dignity within it, personal experience led him 'to accentuate the misogyny that he found in his culture' [159]. This ambivalence matches the ideological contradiction that Johnson found in Milton, between his revolutionary politics and his domestic oppression of women, a contradiction that can readily be given a Marxist gloss [DiSalvo, 1975, 1983; Aers and Hodge, 1981; Quilligan, 1983]. For Quilligan it represents that moment in the seventeenth century when in order to protect patriarchy the bourgeois Protestant revolution needed to exclude women from its libertarian consequences and to establish a new kind of family structure. Milton's emphasis upon Eve's subordination is a response to this social necessity. Far from ignoring female readers, however, to convey this authoritarian message he needs to keep them in mind. In many ways Milton is particularly anxious to speak to female readers above all. What he offers, in return for woman's acceptance of her 'divinely instituted' domestic role, is the reward of an especially attractive affirmation of romantic love. Adam's overriding loyalty to Eve rather than to obedience, Eve's peculiarly important role in the epic, and the 'sexual intimacy of Milton's focus [suggest that] Adam and Eve are of equal importance, if not equal to each other' [239]. This view of sexuality is crucial, because it was recognised in Milton's time that marriage and government were closely related social institutions [Halkett, 1970]. 'Sexuality is political because it is literally the basis of the polis' [Quilligan, 236].

In *Paradise Lost* marriage is shown to be 'the center of social institutions', according to Landy's structuralist-sociological account of kinship systems [1972, 3]. Men and women are prescribed distinct roles: Adam's active, creative, public, while Eve's are domestic, marital and maternal, under his 'natural authority' [5]. To show the contradictions in this portrayal, Landy suggests that before the concept of marriage defines this patriarchal limitation of roles, Eve and Adam were equal because siblings, both children of God. The same kinship principle explodes the poem's other hierarchies, since Satan and Christ are also siblings under God the Father. Yet Satan and Eve (between whom Fish [1967, 249–53] had already drawn parallels) are portrayed as 'deviant' because of their aspirations to achieve equality of role. In Eve's case Milton achieves this suppression by, for instance, portraying her as a mother before he portrays her as a spouse, so that her sphere of action is already limited by this patriarchal designation [6–9]. The textual errors involved in this argument are described by Lewalski [1976], from a liberal humanist standpoint. More important, Landy's scheme of analysis breaks down even in its own terms. In order to present Eve and Adam as siblings as well as sexual partners, for which the text offers no evidence, Landy has to read into them the Eve-Satan parallel (that is, the demonic side of Eve noted by the psychological critics and Henson, 1976). Satan has an incestuous relationship with his daughter-lover Sin, replicated in hers with her son Death. So if Eve 'is' Satan she too must be in an incestuous relationship. But if we were to assent to this simplistic schematism we must also say that God is the grandfather of Sin. If one wishes to ignore the theology of the epic, it is yet difficult to ignore Milton's statement that Eve is 'Daughter of God and Man' [IV 660], which does carry a patriarchal charge but does not suggest Landy's 'fraternal' kinship between Eve and Adam. (Fraternity sounds rather misogynist in a feminist analysis, anyway.) The 'kinship system' begins to look dangerously overloaded. It is questionable that the long-recognised parallel between divine and infernal families can be pushed so far, most readings emphasising rather that the infernal trinity of Satan, Sin and Death is an evil parody of the holy Trinity, its incestuousness signifying spiritual perversion.

Eve's possible deviancy is bound up with her placement in the hierarchy, disobedience essentially being an offence against subordination to God and Adam. But we have already seen that the very notion of Eve's peculiar guilt and deviance is a matter of great contention. That Eve is not 'fallen before the Fall', Lewalski reasserts against Landy; nor is Eve limited to a purely domestic role, for both protagonists share the crucially symbolic activity of gardening, as well as Milton's desiderated 'mutual conversation'. Like Adam she experiences sinless ethical development in Paradise. She is not absent throughout the colloquy with Raphael, nor does she leave because her mental capacities are not equal to it (Milton actually insists that this is not the case: VII 50–1; VIII 48–50). Such arguments are now displacing the traditional assumption that Milton portrays Eve as a more material being than Adam, passion to his reason, intuition to his intellect. That assumption supported the view that Eve's decision to work independently of Adam was effectively the moment of the Fall, since she here flouts the principle of subordination, and is doomed to fall without his stronger intellectual support [Bell, 1953; Burden, 1967, 91]. According to Tillyard, even her Fall was owing only to 'triviality of mind' [260]. A number of feminist critics suggest that in Milton's 'misogynistic' portrayal Eve falls because she moves from Adam's side, and that her major motive in eating the apple represents a similar rebellion against patriarchal authority, a desire to attain equality with Adam and to throw off the prohibitive patriarchal power of God [Gilbert, 1978; Quilligan, 1983; Froula, 1983]. These (both feminist and non-feminist) fatalistic readings of the Separation Scene not only suggest a thoroughly mysogynistic portrayal of Eve, but challenge Milton's emphasis upon free will, for they infer that Eve's departure is presented by Milton as intrinsically wrong. God says that he has made humankind 'Sufficient to have stood, though free to fall' [III 99]. Is Eve not sufficient, then? If so, God planned the Fall. From the premises of free will and God's justice it follows rather that Eve like Adam was an ethically responsible and independent being [Safer, 1972; McColley, 1983]. In the context of Milton's ethic of 'Christian liberty', Eve has a right to make an independent ethical decision. She argues a case for its rationality, and right reason is the basis of Milton's view of responsible action. In particular, she argues that virtue is tested only by temptation, a view supported by Milton's own notions of Christian 'wayfaring' and struggle. Of course, Adam's reply that temptation should not be actively sought is also plausible. But he cannot be criticised for not forbidding Eve to leave him, for such a draconian command would be an offence against 'Christian liberty' [Revard, 1973]. Adam may possess authority, but obedience must not be coerced (just as God does not coerce Eve and Adam into obedience, but leaves them 'free to fall'). As Nyquist [1984] argues, it would be a mistake to read the Separation Scene in such a way as to assign blame. Farwell [1982] remarks that both protagonists are wrong and both are right: it is simplistic to imagine a cause-and-effect relationship between their Separation argument and the Fall. Too much in the epic, from both feminist and theological points of view, hangs on the decision to read the Separation Scene fatalistically. This is, indeed, a textual crux in which feminist and theological arguments – usually seen by unsubtle critics as necessarily opposed to one another – actually work together. To read the scene unfatalistically is not only positive in both feminist and theological terms, but also supported by the poem's discursive practices. For, as Nyquist argues, the scene is presented in a newly dynamic psychological way that prevents uncomplicated interpretive decisions by the reader [209]. This crux is an instance of the wide scope of feminist criticism of *Paradise Lost*, that far from leading to a distortion of Eve's role in the epic (as Lewalski complains), a concern with sexual politics involves fundamental issues in the interpretation of Milton's poem.

Indeed, in McColley's reading it is possible to suggest that

Eve is the poem's major ethical protagonist, since it is she who is most tested, as well as – after the Fall – the first to realise that mutual recrimination is destructive. McColley also extends R. M. Frye's demonstration [1978] that Eve manifests Milton's careful iconographical selection from her traditional portrayals, which suggest that he is representing her much more positively than was usual. Since Milton also rejects 'macho' epic heroism, Quilligan suggests that his domestic emphasis may make Eve the central protagonist of his 'unsung' spiritual heroism [242]. In that light Milton's desire for 'fit' readers [VII 31] necessarily comprehends female readers.

Of those the most significant, for Gilbert [1978], are women writers. From a Bloomian position, she argues that Milton is not only the 'Great Inhibitor' of later poets but also the 'Bogey' of masculinist writing, the patriarchal ideology that prevents women from writing without a sense that they transgress their allotted boundaries. Milton's poem on the great patriarchal myth of Christianity embodies that ideology's male monopoly on writing. In rebelling against it, women writers must identify with Satan's revolt against authority. This identification makes them, like Eve, demonic. In (necessarily) endorsing the Romantic view of Satan as a brave challenger of oppression, Gilbert unblushingly speaks in her own voice of his 'indomitable will and courage' and his championship of liberty and equality [375]. Any number of Miltonists would riposte that Satan is a tyrant, motivated to revolt not by libertarian principles but by the desire for power [IV 40–51]. The rigged debate in book II makes this clear early in the epic. However, Gilbert acknowledges something of the sort (there are several such logical 'slides' in her argument), because she proceeds to argue that Satan is also the epitome of the 'lover and daddy' who oppresses women in a sado-masochistic model of human relationships [378]. In revealing Satan's egalitarian charisma, Milton unconsciously subverts his intentions by giving us a model for female rebellion, but he also (apparently) unconsciously reveals in the Fascist Satan how truly oppressed women are. At different points in Gilbert's argument, then, Milton is unconsciously more misogynistic than he seems, yet unconsciously undermines misogyny. Perhaps this takes Bloomian 'misreading' too far, beyond even those instances where Gilbert quotes Adam's misogynistic speeches after the

Fall as if they were Milton's *in propria persona*. If Milton fully intended Satan to be read as an oppressor, the whole 'unconscious' case rather breaks down, for this particular oppression cannot be taken as justifying patriarchy. As Webber argues, 'Satan is a perfect example of a patriarchal, domineering figure' who can only be taken as a role model if we 'misread and misinterpret Milton' [1980, 16–17]. For Toril Moi, the whole feminist position developed by Gilbert and Gubar [1979] is highly questionable, for they 'persist in defining anger as the only positive signal of a female consciousness', so that the female writer must always be a duplicitous demon [1985, 62]. As for female writers being like Satan, one wonders how many of them would appreciate the idea.

Nevertheless, the relationship of writing to gender is rightly a significant issue for critics of *Paradise Lost*. In Milton's portrayal of poetic inspiration, especially in his first invocation, there are strong sexual overtones [I 1–26; Shawcross, 1976]. A parallel is drawn between the heavenly Muse's nocturnal visits to the poet and the Holy Spirit's impregnation of the world at the Creation [I 21–2, VII 28–30]. Several feminist critics have complained that this represents a male appropriation of the female's exclusive power to give birth, since the image implies a male impregnation by a female power of a male 'womb'. This compounding of feminine into masculine attributes, it is argued, is like Adam's appropriation of the capacity for birth at the creation of Eve [VIII 462–77]. Indeed, Anderson thinks that Eve's nativity from Adam's rib is emphatically made into a scene of childbirth [1986, 137]. But Milton's portrayal of the Muse/Spirit need not, Mollenkott [1978] thinks, necessarily imply male predominance in the imagery. She regards Milton's heavenly Muse as androgynous, just as the word 'brooding' here [I 21] suggests both 'breeding' (masculine) and 'hatching' (feminine). She sees in such images a congruity between Milton's attitudes and that strand of feminist thought which once recommended an androgynous view of gender, subsuming sexual difference. In Davies's account [1986] Milton reclaims 'the feminine principle', in a Jungian sense, within an ideology of androgyny which draws upon Renaissance hermetic lore. Hermeticism revived interest in the notion that the first human being was bisexual, the Fall occurring when the female left the male. Noting recent feminist rejections of the androgynous concept, Farwell [1982] argues that it is dangerous both in feminist terms and in the interpretation of *Paradise Lost*. She cites hermetic accounts of 'the androgynous Adam' which suggest that the feminine principle is merely material and natural while the masculine is mental and spiritual, the dominant element. So even 'androgyny can be seen as a male attempt to appropriate the power of creation for himself' [8]. Interpretatively, the hermetic view of androgyny would suggest that the Fall occurred the moment Eve left Adam, thus breaking up the bisexual compound, and indeed this was a current hermetic reading of Genesis. Transferred to *Paradise Lost*, that allegorical reading gives us the fatalist interpretation of the Separation Scene, that there the Fall is all over bar the shouting. Farwell rejects this, arguing that Milton's reflection of the androgynous Adam and Eve is abandoned after the early books. Eve 'is not ontologically allegorical, but a dynamic and growing individual', as McColley and others have contended [15]. Milton's deliberate adjustment of the androgyny allegory precludes its mysogynistic potential, allowing to Eve and hence generally to 'womankind ... positive possibilities of individuality, separateness, and ... independence' [16]. Relating Eve's portrait to Milton's revolutionary ideology, Webber [1980] eloquently argues that 'Eve reflects every female potentiality that could enter the mind of a Renaissance epic writer and Christian humanist' [1980, 11]. It is, she says, precisely because his avant-garde views so strongly anticipate our own that we have difficulty in reading *Paradise Lost* with equanimity [4]. Were Milton not halfway to feminism, his epic would not be so susceptible to feminist critique.

The prototypical and prescriptive implications of Milton's Eve are consequences of the story he chose. That *Paradise Lost* tells 'the original story', that it stands squarely on claims to Christian and historical truth, are factors deeply involved with the perceived status of Milton's epic. For Gilbert it becomes a 'Bogey'; for Froula [1983] it must be dislodged from the literary 'canon' in an attempt to revise patriarchal systems of evaluation. *Paradise Lost*'s place as 'the great English epic' necessarily makes it also the major target of revisionist critical enterprises. While feminists debate new problems in the text, and refresh the old ones, *Paradise Lost* remains a hot issue.

Part Two
Appraisal

Reading writing in *Paradise Lost*

WHEN Milton claimed that his epic project demanded 'things unattempted yet in prose or rhyme' he explicitly laid claim to immortality. For the first three hundred years of its life *Paradise Lost* has done well enough as immortals go. Readers have seemed, on the whole, to accept Milton's claim to poetic achievement – to literary authority. Before readers and critics regard a work as *literature* rather than merely discourse – that is, any form of writing whether fictive or a shopping list – a writer has to gain acceptance as an author [Foucault, 1986], worthy of explanatory activity by critics and the loving attention of editors. A number of Renaissance poets, Jonson and Milton amongst them, were concerned to construct within their writings a self-image of the 'laureate' which would distinguish them from amateur gentlemen poets [Helgerson, 1983]. Having given frequent notice to readers, in his early poems, of his intention to write something 'so written to aftertimes, as they should not willingly let it die' [*Prose*, II 478], in *Paradise Lost* itself Milton consciously set out to 'overgo' previous epics both classical and modern [pp. 22–5, above]. Milton was, in fact, painfully conscious that his might be 'an age too late' for the writing of an epic poem [IX 44], that the time for such heroic enterprises might have passed. Amongst other things, the distinction of his precursors had raised the stakes, making it more difficult to achieve that originality which was coming to be a requirement of such poetic authority [cf. Guillory, 1983].

Implicit in what I have just said are assumptions about how we measure the claims of an author to literary distinction. Distinction inheres, in this classic view, in priority: the author is the first to achieve a certain literary feat, and in this sense all subsequent writers become belated, that is to say, too late to do what he has done already. That priority is calculable, then, by its effects upon the text's readers, especially upon those who are themselves aspirant authors. In their different ways Marvell, Dryden, Addison and Johnson all agreed in conferring the distinction of priority upon *Paradise Lost*. Equally, later poets recognise that priority by emulating, and failing to free themselves from, his original literary feat: as witness the eighteenth-century experience of Milton. That Milton was an author may seem self-evident, but the establishment of a 'great' poem is not so simple a process. My purpose in this essay is to show how Milton defines the authorship, and hence the 'meaning' of this epic. His method, and its effects, necessarily involve those readers who will decide the poem's literary status. How does he regard – define for himself – his audience? How does he regard himself as an author, and define that authorship for us? What is the role of the reader in accepting these definitions, or rejecting them? How does Milton's imagined audience relate to his actual readership, at the poem's first publication and since, when readers have no doubt changed in the same ways that their culture has altered? We can construct answers to these questions by means of reception theory: that is, the analysis of a text by means of its reading history, the varying ways in which readers have responded to it at different times since its publication. By means of reception and reader-response theories I intend, here, to show how the writer(s) and the reader(s) of *Paradise Lost* are delineated within the text itself. In that portrayal we can locate the way the text constructs an interpretation of the world, and of itself; interpretations which it constructs in consciousness of the readers who will interpret the poem. Essentially, this essay addresses the question: what can its readers tell us about the writing of *Paradise Lost*, and *vice versa*?

According to the reception theorist Jauss [1982], we can account for the diverse interpretations generated by texts by examining the way in which readers have responded to them at various times since their initial publication. Each period in the history of a culture is distinguished by a set of cultural attitudes that varies from those which precede and succeed it. A literary text which was well received at its first appearance and has remained significant was able to satisfy the 'horizon of expectations' which was brought to it by contemporary readers. In order to remain significant, however, the text has to be sufficiently original – sufficiently different from what its readers would normally expect to encounter – to change the horizon of expectations. So, by the mid-eighteenth century Milton's epic had established a norm for the English mode of the 'Sublime', poetry intended to provoke wonder and elevation in its readers. (According to Knott [1984], it is precisely that sense of wonder which we need to recapture in reading Milton now.) In the course of time, cultural and literary change produce changes in the horizon of expectations. As one horizon of expectations is displaced by another, so different interpretations arise of familiar works. One such alteration occurred when the Romantic poets and critics valued Milton rather for his revolutionary fervour than for what previous poets had seen as his unworldly sublimity. They found in Milton what they wanted to find, given their consciously revisionist horizon of expectations.

Initially, of course, *Paradise Lost* was addressed to the audience available in 1667, a readership readily able to recognise its topical references. That contemporary horizon of expectations will be represented, here, by Andrew Marvell's commendatory poem, 'On Mr Milton's *Paradise Lost*', which was printed in the second edition (1674). The two poets were close friends, sharing many reformist religious and political attitudes, including hostility to the restored regime of Charles II. In particular, the apocalyptic elements crucial to Milton's poem [pp. 31–3, above] found a responsive audience in Marvell, who shared the widespread belief in an imminent Second Coming of Christ [Stocker, 1986]. Recognising that *Paradise Lost* portrayed the 'great design' of God's providential plan in history, Marvell gives a dramatic rendition of the astonishing and in some ways disturbing experience of reading this epic for the first time. Was it truly possible for Milton to achieve a poetic 'vast Design' which could be equal to the subject?

> When I beheld the Poet blind, yet bold,
> In slender Book his vast Design unfold
> . . .
>   the Argument
> Held me a while misdoubting his Intent,

> That he would ruine (for I saw him strong)
> The sacred Truths. . .
> (So *Sampson* groap'd the Temples Posts in spight)
> The World o'rewhelming to revenge his Sight.
>   [1–10]

Characterising Milton's poetic heroism, Marvell identifies him
with the protagonist of his *Samson Agonistes* (1671), in which the
blinded hero suicidally destroys the Philistine temple. In this
suggestion of destructive power, sufficient to 'ruine' the great
spiritual mysteries of Milton's biblical source, Marvell plays
devil's advocate by speaking for hostile readers. Milton's
political opponents had taunted him with his blindness [e.g.
'No Blinde Guides', in Parker, 1940], averring that it was a
punishment for his sacrilegious attitude to monarchy. In
Samson Agonistes the blinded Samson is initially resentful that
God should have abandoned him to his enemies – an attitude
which was read as an analogue to Milton's own defeat at the
Restoration. But the play traces his gradual recognition that
God has in fact allotted him a new task, a symbolic defeat of the
Philistines in the very monument to their false religion. Like
Milton's opponents, Marvell pretends to read the play as a
biographical howl of rage, Samson/Milton motivated purely by
personal 'spight' or hatred. In which case, Milton's epic could
be regarded as a false apocalypse, 'The World o'rewhelming';
lacking the objective of true apocalypse, which is to restore
humankind's lost happiness [XII 464–5].

Here Marvell articulates a contemporary recognition of the
religious and political allusions in *Paradise Lost*. In the second
couplet of his poem he achieves a 'ventriloquism' [Gross, 1982,
81] of Milton's voice in the epic's first invocation. There Milton
announces the great span of his theme from the Creation to
Judgement, when man shall 'regain the blissful seat' of the New
Jerusalem [I 1–25]. Throughout the epic Milton maintains the
apocalyptic perspective: most signally at the opening of Book
IV, when as Satan approaches Paradise the narrator wishes
that the devil had been heralded by 'that warning voice, which
he who saw / The Apocalypse heard cry in Heaven aloud' as
the Dragon came to persecute men in the last age of time. In
fact, many contemporary readers believed that they were living
in that last age and suffering the ravages of Antichrist, the

READING WRITING IN PARADISE LOST 63

apocalyptic persona of Satan himself. In the dramatic plot-time of *Paradise Lost* the Latter Days lie in the future, but in the reader's horizon of expectation they could be regarded as current time. Prevailing assumptions regarded the Roman Catholic Church as Antichristian, and to this Milton and Marvell added the corrupt Anglican episcopacy of England. All such corruption finds its archetype in Satan/Antichrist, 'Artificer of fraud . . . the first / That practised falsehood under saintly show' [IV 121–2]. In effect, Antichrist is the embodiment of falsity both religious and political, an enslaver of humankind because Satan is 'slave to himself' and thus subject to a rage for power over others [VI 178–81]. The one angel who resists Satan's subornation, Abdiel, represents at one level the 'saving remnant' of true believers who were thought to persist in godliness despite the Antichristian dominance on earth: 'Among the faithless, faithful only he; / Among innumerable false, unmoved' [v 897–8]. During the War in Heaven, which typologically represents at once the first contest between good and evil and the last, apocalyptic battle [p. 31, above], Abdiel triumphantly displays to Satan the angelic army which manifests the true power of godliness:

> though then
> To thee not visible, when I alone
> Seemed in thy world erroneous to dissent
> From all. My sect thou seest; now learn too late
> How few sometimes may know, when thousands err.
> [VI 144–8]

The key words here are 'dissent' and 'sect', implying that the dissenters and sectarians of Restoration England – like Milton himself and Marvell – are the remnant of true religion. In contrast, Satan's army meets, like the Anglican church, 'in synod' [156]. In the last two Books this confrontation is repeatedly replayed in the course of human history, each age revolving into Antichristian false religion ('idolatry') and government ('tyranny'), against which one single just man (Abraham, Noah: XI 818) stands out. Of these tyrannies Antichrist/Satan is the archetype, his pompous Oriental monarchy signifying the 'false religion' of Islam and a political 'Idol of Majesty' [II 1–6, VI 101]. That Antichristian sway persists until the coming of Christ, the loneliest of all heroes, who in 'a reproachful life and cursed death . . . By his own nation, slain' shall save all [xii 406–14]. At his Second Coming the embattled faithful remnant will finally receive their own release and 'reward', Antichrist having been overcome [xii 445–62]. In this final victory Christ the Judge will be the ultimate 'one just man', of whom Noah is a type [xi 876]. The promise of that release must sustain the faithful few in the meantime. Amongst them is Milton's narrator, self-described as a blind, defeated internal exile in Restoration England.

> fallen on evil days,
> On evil days though fallen, and evil tongues;
> In darkness, and with dangers compassed round
> [vii 25–7]

Recalling Milton's term of imprisonment after the Restoration and his abused sightlessness, these lines encapsulate the hostility which Marvell ventriloquised in his poem. In echoing such opponents while catching the voice of Milton's own invocation, Marvell achieved a dramatic playoff of style against content which implies the potential problems of literary decorum in Milton's own epic. That hostility amongst conservative readers was an accurate response to the implications of Milton's narrative. The various apparently digressive outbursts against false churches and political tyranny which characterise the final Books point in fact to their topical relevance for Restoration England. The biblical history given there is also current time and (in the plot) future time. Then is now, and now is then.

Milton's choice of a biblical subject allowed him to make covert – sometimes dangerously close to overt – topical political reference, without too much interference from the strict censorship exercised in the 1660s. He could always argue that he was imitating the Bible, for which reverence was required (nominally at least) from the censors themselves. If Christ is the true – for Milton the only – king, the Satanic Antichrist is necessarily his false counterpart. Through the Satanic medium Milton can smuggle in his satire on earthly kings, especially in the first two Books, where Satan's role is greatest. On the one hand, the narrator looks forward to human history, when the fallen angels will become Antichristian idols [I 376–521]. On the other, Satan's defiant hogwash about empire and liberty allows for epigrammatic statements by both Satan and the narrator, the universality of which implicitly includes contemporary references also. Any portent in the skies, says the narrator craftily, 'with fear of change / Perplexes monarchs' [I 598–9]; a change, his contemporary readers might think, such as that which robbed Charles I of his throne, and might threaten his son's too, given the various insurgences of the 1660s. Equally, rallying his troops after their defeat, Satan opines that 'who overcomes / By force, hath overcome but half his foe' [648–9]. The Revolution against Charles had succeeded by force of arms, but the Restoration of 1660 showed how partial a victory that had been. Line 1660 of *Samson Agonistes* might well, then, encapsulate that brief triumph: 'O dearly bought revenge, yet glorious!' Milton had indeed paid dearly enough, and the narrator's self-portrait in Book VII of *Paradise Lost* explicitly observes the political hostility of some of his readers, comparing them to 'the barbarous dissonance' of those who tore to pieces the mythic bard Orpheus [32–3]. His polemical writings in the revolutionary period had encountered a similar reaction, 'a barbarous noise' of detractors who prefer comfortable servitude to liberty – like the serfs of tyrant Nimrod in *Paradise Lost* itself [Sonnet XII; *PL* XII 24ff.]. Nevertheless Milton hopes, by the grace of God, to find amongst contemporary readers a minority who will be 'fit audience . . . though few' [VII 31]; a saving remnant, as it were, capable of receiving his reformist message to the nation. Epics were traditionally poems of a national significance, and Milton had early spoken of his ambition to write a work 'doctrinal and exemplary to a nation' [*Prose* II 479].

   Amongst that sympathetic 'fit' audience was, of course, Marvell, and in describing his reading experience of *Paradise Lost* he plays devil's advocate in order to give the hostile reading its due, hence reinforcing the objectivity of his rejecting it. It has been complained that Marvell gives no reasons for his reassurance that Milton's poem is not resentful, irreligious or unsuccessful [Gross, 87]. But before Marvell avows his admiration he has already provided its rationale. The allusion to Samson was deliberately biased in the manner of hostile readers, suppressing Milton's portrait of Samson's election to

his task of destruction by God himself. That election is
implicitly recalled by Marvell's canny connection of it to
apocalyptic ruin. Samson was a type of Christ, selected to
sacrifice himself for his people. A Jewish 'judge' (as Marvell's
allusion here to Judges 16: 29–30 reminds us), Samson also
prefigures Christ as Judge in the Second Coming. In Milton's
play Samson's demolition of the Philistine temple is, then, at
one level the destruction of the false church of Antichrist.
Although Gross [85] has noted that Marvell's use of 'Temple'
here is strange, because it implies a Judaeo-Christian church,
that is precisely what Marvell intends. For him as for Milton,
the contemporary Church in England is Antichristian,
fulfilling the biblical description of Antichrist as one who sits in
the very temples of God himself: false Christianity [2
Thessalonians 2:4]. In his view, Milton like his Samson is a
heroic scourge of the Philistines in contemporary England.
Both look forward to the final vanquishing of Antichristianism
when the world itself is destroyed.

The question remains, for Marvell as for other readers,
whether Milton is right to elect himself as a castigating
prophet, such as he portrays other 'just men' in *Paradise Lost* [XI
812–16]. No doubt that he has the literary qualifications for his
task, a 'mighty Poet' [Marvell, 23] heroic in verse as Samson
was in arms. In locating the source of Milton's literary
strength, though, Marvell also discovers Milton's spiritual
election:

> Where couldst thou Words of such a compass find?
> Whence furnish such a vast expense of Mind?
> Just Heav'n Thee, like *Tiresias*, to requite,
> Rewards with *Prophesie* thy loss of Sight.
>
> [41–4]

Milton has succeeded in his audacious literary project precisely
because he has received that grace of inspiration for which his
invocations pray. Only the 'Heavenly Muse' can inspire
prophecy like that granted to the legendary blind 'Tiresias and
Phineus', 'Those other two equaled with me in fate, / So were I
equaled with them in renown' [*PL* III 19, 33–6]. In this light
Milton's blindness is not malignant but a sign of election, of the
divine gift of foresight which compensated Tiresias and

Phineus for their sightlessness. (Samson's blindness, while a punishment for folly, was also the means whereby he was brought into the heart of the Philistines' temple, because he was no longer considered dangerous.) As a fit reader, Marvell confirms Milton's authority as bardic seer, despite contemporary doubts that there could be modern prophets.

In this endorsement Marvell is, of course, responding to a characterisation which Milton himself has established in his invocations. Like other fictional narrators, Milton's self-projection lays down its own ground rules, represents itself in selective ways. Equally, all narrations contain, as Prince [1980] has observed, a "narratee": the one who receives the narrative, and whom the text also characterises by various indicators or 'markers' within the text itself. As we saw, in the course of presenting himself as a Restoration exile, the narrator divided his audience into the 'fit' and the hostile. Evidently the fit is his intended audience, the hostile here explicitly repudiated by the narrator, as what Culler [1975] would call 'incompetent readers'. Yet evidently there must be also incompetent (that is, unsophisticated) readers who are unable, rather than unwilling, to read this poem 'accurately'. In fact, politically hostile readers were, as we saw, recognising Milton's satirical hits for what they were. So for *Paradise Lost* we can posit several audiences. Within the text, the narratee; amongst its imagined readers, the intended or 'fit audience', the hostile audience, and the merely incompetent audience. (If, as Fish [1967] suggested, Milton deliberately misleads and manipulates his readers, we could describe them as incompetent readers learning to become fit.) However, the narratee in the text does not necessarily correspond to any actual readers, rather to the audience which the text imagines for itself. In which case, the narratee of *Paradise Lost* includes certainly the fit reader, possibly also the (ritually exorcised) hostile reader.

The basic qualification for the narratee, evidently, is that s/he shares the narrator's belief that 'we' are the children of God and of Adam and Eve. Throughout the poem the narratee – Christian Humankind – is addressed through variations on the relevant pronoun. These become particularly frequent as we approach and enter Paradise in Books III and IV, to meet the original human beings, 'our . . . parents' [III 65]. Satan's arrival there is 'our beginning woe' [633]. Those in danger from

him are in the same danger as the narratee, a fact constantly
underlined by such phrases as 'Mother of human race', and,
most shockingly, 'our death' [IV 475, 221]. These implicators,
like those proleptic moments when the narrator pauses to look
forward to the dire consequences of what will happen in
Paradise, are two of the epic's many strategies for bringing
past, present and future into a single textual space. That
simultaneity is most clearly shown in the famous line 'fairest of
her daughters Eve' [324], one of those occasions when the
narrator insists upon the peculiar perspective of the poem. At
one level, of course, such markers are intended to point out that
the poem has religious lessons for its readers, in whatever time.
As Milton had said so many years before, the epic would be
'written *to* after times'. For this reason Addison remarked that
the subject of *Paradise Lost* was of perpetual interest to readers,
since all of us are living out the experience of the Fall [repr. in
Shawcross, 1970, 154]. But the historical dimension of this
claim upon the narratee goes beyond the human perspective, to
the divine overview of history as it moves towards apocalypse.
In God's omniscient view this plan involves a simultaneous
vision of 'past, present, future' [III 78]. In order to present his
'vast Design', to 'justify the ways of God to men' throughout
human history, the epic has to emulate that simultaneous view.
If then is now, and now is then (then can mean either 'in the
past' or 'in the future'), they must remain indistinguishable for
the narratee despite the usual ongoing beginning-middle-end
dynamics of narrative. Narrative order is disrupted anyway in
this epic, which begins in the middle, backtracks to what occurs
immediately before the middle, and then to the beginning of
time itself, before projecting itself forward to the end of the
world. In the course of these toings and froings various
narrators and retrospective narrations interrupt the sequential
plot further. Satan, Adam and Eve all become narratees (of Sin,
of Raphael, of Michael, and in Adam and Eve's case, of each
other's nativity stories too). Within narrations, words like
'then', 'when' and 'now' are made to confuse temporal
distinctions, as is the narrator's use of tenses. When he evokes
the 'voice of St. John's Apocalypse at the opening of Book IV,
the narrator recalls how warning was sounded:

Then when the Dragon, put to second rout,
Came furious down to be revenged on men,
"Woe to the inhabitants on Earth!" that now,
While time was, our first parents had been warned
The coming of their secret foe . . .
. . . for now
Satan, now first inflamed with rage, came down,
The tempter ere the accuser of mankind   [1–10].

Here 'Then when' and 'now . . . now . . . now', with their ambiguous simultaneity, frame that crucial moment when the fate of humankind would alter forever. 'Then' in the first line reflects an allusion to something in the past, the inherited prophecy of John's Revelation, but as prophecy that biblical book used the past tense to describe the future Latter Days. The Dragon will come in that future, yet as a persona of Satan/ Antichrist he is also coming 'now . . . now' to Eden, 'inflamed' with revenge just as the Dragon will later be an avenging scourge of humankind at the apocalypse [4, 9–11]. Within this past-future compounding of Satanic hatred lies the narratee's own time, 'now' also referring to his/her reading present, when in spiritual form other Satanic avatars daily 'tempt' humankind to sin. The wages of that sin, like (and following) the first Fall mentioned here, will become apparent at the Last Day, when Satan the tempter becomes humankind's accuser too: doubly malignant, even as he is here doubly portrayed as Dragon and fallen angel. The spiritual linkage, the eternal single battle between good and evil, is signified by the allusions to the two battles of apocalypse [3] and Satan's loss of the 'first battle' in heaven [12]. In spiritual terms time is an eternal present, just as God sees it thus. So here the narrator explicitly draws together the complicated to-and-fro time scheme of the whole poem. The first battle is yet to come, in Book IV; the 'second rout' is forecast by the apocalyptic history of Books XI–XII; the temptation itself in Book IX; Satan/Dragon's fall already effected in Book I and replayed in Book VI. As the narrator presses upon the narratee with reiterated 'nows' [5, 8, 9, 16, 23, 27, 30], we are approaching the great original temptation which is replayed in the soul of every believer throughout human history. Even, 'now', within the soul of the narratee, whether s/he will be 'fit' and understand this spiritual challenge issued by the narrator, or unfit and purblind. Like St John, the narratee must now 'see' 'The Apocalypse' [1–2] if the current relevance of temptation is to be understood. This moment of Satan's approach is the beginning of that End for humankind, for all narratees.

So within the framing 'Then . . . now' ambiguity of this passage [1–5, matched by 'now . . . / Then' in 30–1 at the close], the narrator further interinvolves the time-scheme by a confusion of tense-indicators: 'saw . . . Then when . . . second . . . came . . . now, / While time was, our first . . . coming . . . scaped . . . came down . . . ere . . . first battle . . . begins . . . the birth . . . Now' [1–16]. Elements within this compounding provide answering balance to one another, the 'Apocalypse' preceding the 'birth' of Satan's plot against mankind, though the former is the end of the plot; the 'second' coming of Satan/Dragon precedes, here, his 'first'; the 'second' defeat precedes the 'first'; their progeny, mortal 'men', precede 'our first parents'. Then the complementarity of these times pivots round, and Satan is first tempter and after accuser of humankind, in normal temporal sequence. That sequence is then overthrown again, as we are told to remember Satan's initial defeat in Heaven, which refers back to that 'Apocalypse' (later in time but earlier in the passage) when he will be defeated again. This deliberate temporal confusing of the narratee moves, as the narrator introduces Satan's soliloquy, into a similar treatment of place. Already we have, in the course of these opening lines, flitted rapidly between heaven, earth, and hell, with their various examples of the one great war between good and evil. As Satan makes his speedy journey from Heaven to Paradise [12–13], the narrator underlines another example of spiritual simultaneity. Despite his frenetic movement, Satan is locked in the perpetual stasis of egotistic evil. For him all places, like all times, are the same: his malignity

> like a devilish engine back recoils
>   Upon himself . . .
> The Hell within him, for within him Hell
> He brings, and round about him, nor from Hell
> One step no more than from himself can fly
> By change of place.

[17–23]

Already the narratee has been reminded of the circular nature of Satan's experience, from defeat in heaven at the beginning of time to defeat on earth at the end. Evil is, in time as well as psychologically, self-reflexive, self-defeating, 'recoils / Upon himself'. This is the obverse of God's simultaneous omniscience, a perpetual banal horror in which time and place are ever the same. For this purpose Satan's arrival and soliloquy are related in the historical present: 'Begins his dire attempt. . .' [15f.]. This, too, refers to the present of the narratee ['Now . . . now', 16–23], who is also capable of experiencing the psychological trap of evil. As we enter Eden, seeing it from the perspectives of both the narrator and Satan, we have been taught to see the invasion as our test too. And in the warning note of danger, the apocalyptic perspective has also reassured the narratee of God's triumphant plot, an ultimate rescue. Fear and an implied (if also apocalyptically terrible) reassurance mix there, in the simultaneity of then/now vision. The simultaneity of the text exists at all levels: dramatic, structural, doctrinal, moral, historical, psychological. In other words, it inheres in the relation of narrator and narratee, as controlled by deictics of time and place.

Here the sketching of God's eternal plot – the providential plan which will 'justify his ways to men' – reflects his nature as 'the world's great Author' [v 188], the original voice for whom the narrator is only (he hopes) a medium. God's counterpart is Satan the 'Author of all ill', false plotter, hypocrite and thus false speaker, of 'glozing lies' [II 381, III 93]. The narrator, as a fallible man, lies between the two, subject to Satanic suggestion like Eve despite his prayers for heavenly inspiration. In 'evil days' he is surrounded by 'evil tongues', who even if he writes of truth aright will deliberately misread and mispeak him.

Heroic writing?

Given the alterations in the horizon of expectations which have occurred since the passing of Milton's 'fit audience', what can later readers, like Johnson and the modern Satanists, tell us about the writing of *Paradise Lost*? While the contemporary audience can tell us a great deal about what Milton's intention was taken to be then, from the perspective of the 1980s we have to recognise that the interpretation of *Paradise Lost* has a historical aspect also. Readers now inherit all the readings which have been made in the past, so that (for instance) the Satanist reading is a known element which we bring to the poem rather than gain *from* it. Whether or not the Satanist reading is 'true' does not much matter, in the sense that we cannot avoid being aware of this possibility in the poem. Because modern interpretations always include a consciousness of previous interpretations, we cannot recapture the impact of the epic upon its first readers. We cannot be innocent readers. The best example of our inheritance of earlier readers' views (our inheritance, like humankind in Milton's poem, of 'original sin' so to speak) is the pervasive influence of Johnson's critique. Surprisingly, Johnson is still the most influential critic of *Paradise Lost*. This is most true where it is least expected. A peculiarly telling example is Gilbert's feminist reading, where she quotes Virginia Woolf's as the reaction to the poem peculiar to women writers/readers [1978, 370; see p. 56, above]. But in her complaint, 'Has any great poem ever let in so little light upon one's own joys and sorrows?', Woolf is consciously or unconsciously echoing Johnson's, that the reader 'has . . . little natural curiosity or sympathy' because the poem does not touch his/her own experience [106]. So it is at least dubious that this reaction represents a peculiarly feminine response to Milton's poem. At any rate, it was manifestly Johnson who first and most forcibly expressed those problems which have continued to perplex later readers.

Himself a victim of severe religious fears, and conscious of his own failings, Johnson found Milton's massive confidence in his own election to grace intimidating [Griffin, 1986, 213]. While this confidence was an absolute prerequisite of Milton's ability to undertake the literary prodigy of *Paradise Lost*, equally Johnson was disturbed by its overtones of hubris. Again and again he underscores Milton's arrogance, both personal and literary. Indeed, while Milton chose the largest possible subject and proved equal to it, yet this was the only subject that could 'satiate his appetite of greatness' [103]. That observation implies at once the heroism of Milton's poetic stance (Johnson indeed calls him a hero) and the appalling conceit which made it possible. Appalling, for Johnson, because Milton here sets out to describe the indescribable, to tread on the very margin of blasphemy. Johnson himself refuses to discuss God and Christ in their capacity as 'characters' of the poem. His attitude may seem quaint to a modern reader, but Johnson's religious sensibility was a good deal closer to that of Milton's contemporaries than ours could be, especially as Johnson was somewhat old-fashioned in his religious attitudes even then. It is safe to assume that Milton himself was well aware of the possible spiritual dangers of his project. Nuttall [1980] wonders how a poet who truly believes can put words into God's mouth without shuddering at his own temerity. We have only to recall the many critics who have complained of Milton's 'full frontal' depiction of God [pp. 19–20, above] to admit, without further argument, that Milton does put words into his God's mouth, some of them theologically controversial. This blatant god-making, this deliberate evocation of religious issues by God himself in Milton's text, seems very odd if we consider that for Milton God can only speak the truth. How is Milton to decide truth? He himself argued in *Areopagitica* that no one had a monopoly on truth in our puzzled postlapsarian world, only the right to investigate it sincerely and honestly. Yet Milton does claim, through the mouth of his God, to speak the absolute truth. In that sense, as the author of God's words in this text, he does what Abdiel accuses Satan of doing: 'Shalt thou give law to God. . .?' [v 822]. Satan deliberately misrepresents God's decrees, but Milton the author is not really in a better case, since (as a postlapsarian man, in his own view at least) he is incapable of representing God's truth. In a postlapsarian universe, such as Milton the poet and his intended audience inhabit, God is 'Unspeakable. . . . invisible' [v 156–7].

Like Adam after the Fall, we have lost the right to converse directly with God: 'This most afflicts me, that . . . from his face I shall be hid, deprived / His blessed countenance . . . Presence Divine' [xi 315–19]. Before the Fall man could encounter God, in the person of the Son, face to face. God was then seeable as well as (so to speak) talkable, whereas he is now unspeakable because invisible, not recognisable or describable. This is not merely, in Milton's text, because God withdraws from man after the Fall, but also because language itself, the medium of description and communication, was corrupted by the Fall. 'For understanding ruled not, and the will / Heard not her lore' [ix 1127–8]. In Book ix action first becomes contrary to semantic expression: Adam and Eve make physical love but descend into verbal recrimination. There is an oblique relationship, no longer an exact relationship, between what they do and what they say. Sexual intercourse, once the purest physical expression of their mutual accord, now in its lustful postlapsarian form is an index of their alienation from each other's whole selves, of their relation as *merely* physical beings. Physical intercourse is now an action which, contrary to appearances, signifies separation; equally, their verbal quarrel shows their mutual guilt, their enforced community in distress [1187–9]. At this moment they are already demonstrably in the power of Satan, a power they have themselves conferred upon him by accepting as truth his 'glozing lies'. The disparity between speech and action which characterises this episode shows that humankind has now assumed the Satanic state of being. This newly fallen and fallacious mode of existence contrasts with humankind's Edenic state, in which words and things accurately reflected each other: discourse was (as it were) real, embodied in what it described: true. Adam was then able to attach accurate labels to the creation: 'I named [the animals] as they passed, and understood / Their nature' [VIII 352–3]. In the postlapsarian state truth is difficult to distinguish from falsity, yet false may sometimes obliquely signify true – just as Adam and Eve's fallen lust accurately symbolised their miserably alienated state. In this light, language becomes an index of God's mercy, for even after the Fall Adam and Eve are allowed to converse with the Son one last time, face to face. The very occurrence of such an encounter, even though it includes the announcement of their punishment, sufficiently indicates that all is not yet lost, and prefigures that moment when, the postlapsarian world having been destroyed, humankind shall see God again at the end of time: 'revealed / In glory' [XII 545–6].

To see the Son is also to see the Word, since Christ is the embodied truth-speech of God [John 1:1]. By this Word, this command which is also a presence, the world is created [VII]. Visible and sayable are thus, in *Paradise Lost*, the same thing. For God at least, who *is* truth. But in *Paradise Lost* visible and sayable are, equally, not the same thing at all. For every word in the text is attributable to a human source, the author or narrator, who necessarily exists in the postlapsarian condition in which speech and its referents are problematically divorced. This point is the basis of all Milton's problems in writing, whether religious or literary. No matter how much critical ingenuity is expended on solving them [e.g. Kerrigan, 1974; Lieb, 1981], and this has been considerable, I think we must simply admit at once that Milton's problems are not in any actual sense solvable. Given his own beliefs, he cannot portray God adequately; cannot make God speak, or portray cosmological wonders beyond human ken, without risking blasphemy, displaying temerity, and jeopardising 'truth'. He had to extend a few scriptural verses in Genesis into a long poem without fictionalising religious truth or seeming to attempt to improve on the Bible – unimprovable, for Milton and his intended audience, because it is the revelation given by God himself. Stated simply, indeed, Milton's problem is that he must not fictionalise the truth [Crossman, 1980, 136–61], but he cannot avoid doing so because the epic is a literary text. Milton's intended audience understood this paradox, as Marvell shows when he worries that Milton will sacrifice divine truth 'to Fable and old Song' [8]. Given that *Paradise Lost* is necessarily for both author and intended reader a fallen fiction pretending to truth, how can Milton hope to give adequate expression to the absolute necessity, for him, of justifying God's ways to men? 'How may I express thee unblamed?' [III 3]. He cannot simply evade the problem, pretend that it does not exist, for this would compound the fault. The one thing he can do is to stress the fault, to open up a ravine of uncertainty in the text into which the reader will fall with his/her eyes open. Although claiming the status of literary authorship, the text must display the tenuousness of its spiritual authority. Fiction must admit its fictionality, its inadequacy; yet, somehow, the truth must be a *felt* absence, something conceivable even if unsayable. The poem, like postlapsarian consciousness itself, must be 'darkness visible'. Who better to embody this than Milton himself, our blind guide to the truth? Or rather, Milton's self-projection, the narrator who is a blind bard.

Accordingly, at the narrator's first appearance the prayer for divine inspiration, for the authority to speak truth, involves an equally emphatic reference to blindness, both physical and spiritual. 'What is me is dark / Illumine' [I 22–3]. As we have seen, Milton's contemporary readers were divided (politically at least) between those who located in his blindness a god-given sign of his unfitness for the task, and those who discovered in it divine election to true prophecy. Indeed, Milton himself had been forced to contemplate the spiritual meaning of his affliction: 'I call . . . God to witness . . . that I am not conscious of any offence, though to the utmost of my power I have often seriously examined myself on this point . . . which . . . could have called down this calamity upon me' [Diekhoff, 1939, 98–9]. If, in the narrator of *Paradise Lost*, this ambiguity were embodied, were carefully signalled to the narratee, then Milton's text would not be foreclosing the question of religious authority. To pray for inspiration within the text would signal the question of whether it had been vouchsafed or not; especially if, as in the very first invocation, the narrator confessed to his spiritually problematic blindness. To fashion the narrator so obviously would, for the narratee, explicitly place on trial the text's authority. Constant address of the narratee, direct or oblique, would maintain the reader's sense of the text's construction, its objectives, its problems. So, in Book IV, the frequent apostrophe to the narratee implied by the implicatives 'we' and 'our' is reinforced by the narrator's increasingly obvious presence. The famous narrative outburst on the subject of 'wedded love', challenging common assumptions about the inherent evil of sex, is further pointed by the narrator's explicit self-instruction: 'Far be it that I should write thee sin or blame, / Or think thee unbefitting holiest place' [IV 758–9]. As the syntax forcefully indicates to the reader, to 'write' something is to make it – to make the evil which is 'sin or blame' rather than the good which is truth. Like God the just, the fallible narrator is yet spiritually responsible for what he undertakes to create. As the moment of the Fall approaches, the narrator's invocation to Book IX signals the greatest alteration in terms of language itself:

> No more of talk where God or angel guest
> With man,
> . . . permitting him the while
> Venial discourse unblamed. I now must change
> Those notes to tragic

[IX 1–6]

We have lost the world of discourse where Adam and God could discuss man's desire for converse (in all senses) with a partner, as Adam had asked the Son for his Eve; where Raphael could converse with Eden's inhabitants. The loss of harmony is the loss of mutuality, of communion and communication, in which 'Venial discourse unblamed' was possible. So, too, the narrator, who had prayed for the ability to 'express thee unblamed', 'must change' to a genre and a mode of discourse which fully reflect fallen disillusionment. The notion of his compulsion by fallen conditions records his own implication, in writing, in this spiritual infection. That reminder is counterbalanced by his commitment to sing the true Christian heroism, rather than the warlike subjects usually deemed the proper concern of epic and romance, 'fabled knights / In battles feigned' [30–1]. Christian valour, 'which justly gives heroic name / To person or to poem. Me. . .' [40–1]: that juxtaposition of the narrator's self with hero and heroic epic is a reading clue to his courage in confronting the tragedy of Fall, striving to describe adequately something by which he himself is compromised. Unless the heavenly Muse aids him, any number of contingencies – timing, age, an uncongenial place in Restoration England, themselves the time-bound conditions of fallen humankind – may 'damp my intended wing' [44–5]. The image of the poet in song-flight looks back to the very first invocation, reminding the narratee of the poet's brave intentions. 'Invoke thy aid to my adventurous song, / That with no middle flight intends to soar . . . while it pursues / Things unattempted yet' [i 13–16]. Now some way into this heroic poetic performance, the narratee is reminded to judge how far that promise has been sustained. For it was at once a literary and a spiritual promise, to be 'heroic' both in epic form and in the recovery of truth from fallen vision. Evidently both Johnson and Marvell, in acknowledging Milton's heroism, responded to the implied question in the affirmative.

That literary heroism involves, like all courageous enterprises, risk. Milton's many forecasts, in his early works, that he would attempt the great work, would now appear merely embarrassing had he (like his contemporary Cowley) failed to produce it. That literary wager – conscious of the odds of belatedness, arrogance, an unresponsive audience – is matched, in spiritual terms, by the narrator's wager on faith.

For Pascal, belief was itself a wager on God. So does this narrator embark on a feat of spiritual danger, presuming to portray God and his truth despite all the human fallibilities represented by his blindness. Without his guide, the Holy Spirit, his flight will fail, and 'on the Aleian field I fall, / Erroneous there to wander and forlorn' [vii 19–20]. If he does fail, he will replicate in himself, in writing, the original Fall. In blind indirection, he will be like the expelled Adam and Eve: 'wandering . . . their solitary way' through the wilderness of a world from which God has withdrawn his presence, his presentness to sight [xii 648–9].

In this alienation from God's sight, as also in his boast of a daring undertaking, the narrator's one counterpart within the narrative is (strangely) Satan: another author. Against this sinister parallel, this embodiment of the false speaking and fake authority to which the narrator himself may succumb, the invocations repeatedly announce the narrator's lack of self-sufficiency, his need for God's authorisation by inspiration. But, equally, as the narrator embarks upon this risky poem the Satanic parallel is signalled with considerable force. Riggs [1972, 15–45] suggests that there are a number of curious likenesses between Milton and Satan in the early books. If so, we might take these as narrative signals, an aspect of the narrator's self-presentation which maintains a constant pressure upon the narratee to remember the limitations and dangers of postlapsarian writing. This poem may indeed be the 'true fortitude' the narrator hopes for, or it may be a Satanic flight and fall, the self-raising in which aspiration converts to pure egotism. In this light 'my adventurous song' [i 13] carries *all* the connotations of adventure – risk, courage, danger, possibly foolhardiness, certainly an exposure to the unknown. These are, of course, precisely the terms in which Satan boasts of his journey through Chaos to earth and the great enterprise of ruining humankind. His initial revolt, too, was as 'ambitious' as it was 'impious' [i 41–3]; the narrator's aspiration similarly ambitious and, perhaps, impious: 'Into the Heaven of Heavens I have presumed, / An earthly guest' [vii 13–14], as he will later emphasise to the narratee, referring to the Holy Council and the War in Heaven [iii, vi]. Of earthly scenes 'More safe I sing with mortal voice' [vii 23–4], with less spiritual hazard, that is, both to the narrator and the narratee whom he might mislead.

But those hazards, the great chasm of uncertainty which must open up before the reader if such misleading is to be honestly present as a textual potential, have to be definitely established right at the start.

In the first two books that Satanic possibility is firmly indicated. Like the blinded narrator on earth, Satan in the Hell of the mind sees 'No light' – the light of God's enlightenment – 'but rather darkness visible' [I 63, 73]. Like the narrator in the preceding invocation, Satan sees his initial aspiration/rebellion as a 'glorious enterprise', 'That with the mightiest raised me to contend' [89, 99]. Just so has our epic narrator explicitly striven with the mightiest writers of ancient and modern times, announcing his intention to overgo their achievements [16]. In Satan, and in man, such arrogance is 'Disobedience' to the one true authority, presuming 'to have equaled the Most High' [40]. So Satan claims the divine serenity, the ultimate timelessness and changelessness: 'A mind not changed by place or time' [253]. In due course we will see that this is the false image of the true, Satan's changelessness really the stasis of evil frustrating itself. But at this point his is dangerously close to the narrator's aspiration to survey the whole span of time from Creation to End [1–5], to imitate the divine simultaneity of 'then and now'. Meanwhile, the narrator explicitly interrupts Satanic rhodomontade with signals of God's overview and control: 'high permission of all-ruling Heaven / Left him at large to his own dark designs' [212–13; cf. 241]. As Hartman suggests, God's counterplot ironically overlays Satanic plotting [1965; cf. p. 48, above]. Behind the 'darkness visible' of Hell, and of the blind man's storytelling, lies the 'invisible glory' of God the ultimate author [369–70]. In Satan's loud presence the narratee confronts the embodiment of clouded vision, obscuring also in his activities here the unseen brightness of deity. All fallen beings, including the one who narrates this scene, live like the Sons of Belial in that self-made blindness or night [500–1]. For fiction, as artifice, is an art the devils share, and all artificers should 'Learn how their greatest monuments of fame, / And strength and art are easily outdone / By spirits reprobate' [695–7]. So says the narrator, with conscious or unconscious ironic reflection upon his own claim to literary distinction. Ability, ingenuity and industry, such as demons have, is not enough for this poem, which demands a writing in the spirit. Without that, the narrator's are 'proud imaginations' [II 10] like Satan's. Indeed, Johnson receded with horror from such elements in *Paradise Lost*. Given the insistent Satanic parallels here, however, we might well conclude that Johnson was accurately reading signals sent by the text itself. If so, his resistance to the religious sublime in this epic ironically represents an effective outcome of a narrative strategy whereby the narrator jeopardises his own authority. Similarly, to take a later reader, Tillyard's opinion that Milton identified with Satan's 'heroic energy' is a response evoked by the text's flickering equation between Satan's and the narrator's heroic ventures in plotting. Such sceptical readings are appropriately evoked by a self-deconstructing narrative.

Understanding the demolitionary potential of Milton's attempt to build a poetic 'vast Design', Marvell perhaps remembered the narrator's self-presentation in Satanic guise, the devil's 'bold design' of a revenge plot against the first plotter [I 385–6]. While Satan boasts that he is the man for 'aught . . . Of difficulty or danger' [II 447–9], Johnson as a responsive reader understood the implicit comparison, even if he was not conscious of how the narrator had dictated it to him: the author of *Paradise Lost*, he says, 'was born for whatever is arduous' [113]. Such Satanic parallels are translated into action as Satan's flight through the great darkness echoes the narrator's intention in poetry, and seems to require the same qualifications – fitness, an ability to find direction rather than wander lost in uncharted territory:

> . . . whom shall we send
> In search of this new world, whom shall we find
> Sufficient? who shall tempt with wandering feet
> . . .
> And through the palpable obscure find out
> His uncouth way, or spread his airy flight
> Upborne with indefatigable wings
> . . .
> . . . . . what strength, what art can then
> Suffice. . .?
>
> [II 403–11]

As well as the insistent parallels with the narrator's soaring flight in the first invocation, and Marvell's description of Milton's wing as 'indefatigable', readers might also recall his characterisation of his immature talents in *Lycidas*, where the 'uncouth' poet attempted a work for which he confessed himself unripe [1–3]. Indeed, by the time of writing this epic, his blindness ironically could figure precisely that uncharted realm of invisible truth in which he might lose himself, spiritually at least. So Satan 'the void profound / Of unessential Night receives. . . / Wide gaping, and with utter loss of being threatens him' [II 438–41]. The paradoxical self-dissolution of evil selfishness is here fully figured, in its loneliness and spiritual death. If comparable to the hazards embarked on by the narrator, these at once encode both the potential spiritual disaster and the heroism of his attempt to speak in God's language: both courage and its pitfalls obliquely represented by the Satanic voyage.

So, introducing that journey, the demons' pastimes evoke the false image of sacred song. Inflamed with 'false presumptuous hope' by Satan's daring [522], some occupy themselves with a 'song' which because demonic is 'partial', not true [552]. Others speculate upon matters hidden, 'reason[ing] high / Of providence, foreknowledge, will, and fate . . . And found no end, in wandering mazes lost' [555–61]. Such a false 'eloquence' represents the obverse of what the narrator hopes to achieve in his epic of God's mysterious providence; just as the demons' 'bold adventure to discover wide / That dismal world' [571–2; cf. 615] reflects the possibly erroneous course of his own 'adventurous song' – a journey which may also become 'lost' in the 'mazes' of impious speculation. Such narrative inflections should colour the narratee's reaction to the Satanic 'solitary flight', 'with thoughts inflamed of highest design' [630–2] such as the narrator's own. Shortly, Satan encounters in Sin the embodiment of his own plot against the Creation: 'Thou art my father, thou my author' [864]. 'Author of evil, unknown till thy revolt, / Unnamed in Heaven' [VI 262–3], Satan is originator of the very concept and hence of the word. 'Evil, be thou my good' [IV 110]. He is a false author because a false seer, all things distorted by his megalomaniac perspective. He cannot recognise his own 'writing', Sin, because he cannot see his own evil: 'I know thee not, nor ever saw till now/Sight more detestable', even though Sin is his own 'perfect image' [II

744–5, 764]. Their relationship, as of writer to written, parodies the true image of God's Word in the Son [III 384–6]. That false seeing and hence false writing is what the narrator hopes to avoid. Although even in Eden Satan 'Saw undelighted all delight' [IV 286], one of the narrator's many intrusive sermons to the narratee in this Book has already suggested the moral ambiguity of sight:

> . . . So little knows
> Any, but God alone, to value right
> The good before him, but perverts best things
> [201–3]

In this Book, indeed, the narrator by such means begins to open up a distance between Satan's adventure and his own, moving closer to his originators and 'ours', 'our parents', to the 'true authority' exercised by Adam before the Fall corrupted all authority. In that, as another 'image of their glorious Maker', Adam like the Son represents the true word of God [292–5]. He is, as Eve says (correcting the false image of written to writer which her hellish counterpart, Sin, earlier expressed to her own author), 'My author and disposer' [635]. From God through the Son to Adam and Eve and their own unfallen prayers, the essential Word remains uncorrupted through all its images. In that paradisal unanimity of word and truth the narrator points to what he cannot himself recapture. But he is also preserved from the Satanic inability to see aright, for he cannot see at all. In that lies the potential for an inspired seer-bard, who is able only to see what is invisible. If, unlike other men, he cannot observe the seasons, nor the features of his location [III 40–50], to the same degree he may be able like God to see beyond the presentness of time and place, to the undifferentiated 'then is now' of providential omniscience. In which case 'I may see and tell / Of things invisible to mortal sight' [54–5].

In that respect the narrator is discriminated from Satan, who is the epitome of presumptuous seeing, a curiosity about matters hidden which will mislead Adam and Eve also. All are thus transgressors, just as Satan is a 'spy' [II 970]. His journey is a trespass beyond the boundaries of his allotted abode in hell, the fugitive adventure of a spy into forbidden territory. God himself observes 'what rage *transports* our Adversary' 'whom no bounds . . . can hold' [III 80–4]. The blatant pun gives signal to the narratee of what a trespasser's journey represents: in Satan's own words, 'Unspeakable desire to see, and know' [662] what God has denied. The narrator and Adam both display a similar urge to know and say and see the unknowable, which for Adam and Eve becomes the 'adventure' of the Fall. As such, it is prefigured in Eve's dream, when the 'venturous arm' of the Tempter plucks the fruit [v 64]. While this venture is a transgression against God's single word of prohibition, equally it will precipitate the vitiation of all postlapsarian language. And this is truly an (ad)venture, because in eating Adam and Eve choose an unknown future – what will be the lonely and indeed fatal adventure on which they embark at the end of the poem.

Throughout the epic, in fact, heroic similes of the classical type evoke journeys great and small, prosperous and disastrous. Satan's landing leads to a comparison with the astronomer's mapping of the heavens [III 588ff.]. As he approaches Eden, the pleasant climate comes as a relief, like that experienced by sailors venturing 'Beyond the Cape of Hope' [IV 159ff]: so is Satan gone beyond hope into a raging despair. Since his journey is transgressive, the comparison is superseded by his characterisation as the Antichrist who infiltrates the Temple of God: 'So clomb this first grand thief into God's fold; / So since into his church lewd hirelings climb' [192–3]. When Eve and Adam themselves become transgressors after his example, they search for foliage to cover the shame of their nakedness: covering the image of God which the narrator told us was 'unblamed', becoming concealers and hypocrites, false beings and false speakers like Satan. No longer godlike but primeval 'savage[s]', they evoke comparison with the American Indians discovered by Columbus [x 1085, 1115–18], who some contemporaries had thought might represent something close to the original Edenic state. Like Columbus, the narrator himself has embarked in earlier books upon a voyage to discover primal innocence, something unknown to his and the narratee's postlapsarian consciousness.

The relevance of such similes to the world of the contemporary reader, their address to the narratee's current experience, is readily signified by allusions to the newly improved art of navigation, and the newly-discovered lands to which they gave access – like the 'new world' which Satan set out to find [II 403]. These reflect the hazards of human life in its fallen form, as represented by the lonely wayfaring of Adam and Eve in the wilderness of this world. That finale is also the beginning of the kind of life narratees experience, a 'then is now' in which text and actuality might merge. Equally, though, it is there announced that 'Providence [is] their guide', just as the narrator hopes for heavenly guidance in his own uncharted journey into sacred mysteries, a poetic journey in which he professes to guide his own narratee. If the narrator has asked to be the narratee of God, of his truth, then his own relationship to the narratee rightly evokes his uncertainties. His doubts are marked out so that they might become our doubts of him. If guidance prevails, the heroic journey, whether spiritual or literary, will avoid the 'erroneous' (i.e., erring as in wandering without direction, as well as spiritually straying from the true path) possibilities and become a triumphant voyage of discovery – the discovery of the truth that lies behind appearances, like the unknown lands which lay behind the blank areas on early maps. The narrator–narratee relationship, which explicitly marks out the navigations of the text, is the cartography of spiritual enterprise. Writing, as inscribed in this relationship, is itself the sacred if necessarily indeterminate project of *Paradise Lost*. Its readers' reactions can, in this light, be seen to represent that very process of searching for the 'Lost' space in human history. In their critiques, the early readers Marvell and Johnson significantly fall into echoes of the text itself, evidencing their own acquiescence in the role of narratee. The narrator spoke, in Belial, of his own creative potential: 'who would lose, / Though full of pain, this intellectual being, / Those thoughts that wander through eternity. . .?' [II 146–8]. Responding like a perfect narratee, Johnson at once reproves and delights in that expedition of the mind:

> Milton's delight was to sport in the wide regions of possibility; reality was a scene too narrow for his mind. He sent his faculties out upon discovery into worlds where only imagination can travel.   [103]

As necessity is the mother of invention, so blindness releases imagination. The narrator's characterisation as an embattled and lonely dependant of God's guidance is a self-fashioning after Adam's own spiritual discovery: 'on him sole depend, / ... by things deemed weak / Subverting worldly strong' [XI 564–7]. Once, meditating upon his blindness, Milton had claimed that 'in proportion as I am weak, I shall be invincibly strong', a vessel of divine enlightenment [*Prose* I 239; 2 Corinthians 12:9]. In fact, since his disability forced Milton to dictate rather than write, this poem more closely imitates God's authorship of the world by speech: 'my Word, begotten Son . . . speak thou, and be it done' [VII 163–4]. As in God's authorship there is no problematic distinction between what is said and what is done, so there are no temporal distinctions between them: 'His Word . . . Immediate are the acts of God, more swift / Than time'. Whereas the human narrator is committed perforce precisely to the temporality of narration, 'process of speech' [175–8]. The narrator asks for that simultaneity, an 'unpremeditated verse' which recaptures the prelapsarian immediacy of 'unmeditated . . . prompt eloquence' [IX 24, v 149]. The poem's temporal image of that coincidence of speech and truth, divine and human, is the future apocalypse, when Heaven and Earth become one Paradise [XII 463–5]. Time and place are then dissolved, and humankind, once more able to see God, will embark on a different adventure, begun by Christ's second advent. At this sighting (or dis-covering) of the last Word, narrator and narratee will make the final discovery, of 'another world' [XI 877] altogether.

References

Critical works cited in this book are listed below. In terms of critical approach, some belong in more sections than one. Any individual critic's work is best located by means of the Index. Names preceded by an asterisk denote the compilers of collections of essays, listed below.

Collections of Essays

Barker, A. E., *Milton: Modern Essays in Criticism* (London and New York, 1965).

Dyson, A. E. and Lovelock, J., *'Paradise Lost', A Casebook* (London, 1973).

Fiore, A. P., *Th'Upright Heart and Pure* (Pittsburgh, 1967).

Franson, J. K., *Milton Reconsidered* (Salzburg, 1976).

Kermode, F., *The Living Milton* (London, 1960).

Kranidas, T., *New Essays on 'Paradise Lost'* (Berkeley, 1969).

Patrides, C. A., *Approaches to 'Paradise Lost'* (Toronto, 1968).

Rajan, B., *'Paradise Lost': A Tercentenary Tribute* (Toronto, 1969).

Rudrum, A., *Milton: Modern Judgements* (Nashville and London, 1970).

Introduction

Adams, R. M., *Ikon: Milton and the Modern Critics* (Ithaca, NY, and London, 1955).

Eliot, T. S., *Milton* (London, 1968, reprint of 1936 and 1947 essays).

Griffin, D., *Regaining Paradise: Milton and the Eighteenth Century* (Cambridge and New York, 1986).

Gross, K., ' "Pardon Me, Mighty Poet": Versions of the Bard in Marvell's "On Mr Milton's *Paradise Lost*', *Milton Studies* 16 (1982) pp. 77–95.

Havens, R. D., *The Influence of Milton on English Poetry* (Cambridge, Mass., 1922).

Leavis, F. R., *Revaluation* (1936; repr. Harmondsworth, 1972), pp. 46–65.

Murray, P., *Milton: The Modern Phase* (London, 1967).
Parker, W. R., *Milton's Contemporary Reputation* (Columbus, 1940).
Raleigh, W., *Milton* (London and New York, 1900).
Samuel, I., *'Paradise Lost'*, in Lumiansky, R. M., and Baker, H. (ed.), *Critical Approaches to Six Major English Works* (Philadelphia, 1968), pp. 209–53.
Saurat, D., *Milton: Man and Thinker* (1925; rev. edn. London and New York, 1944).
Shawcross, J. T., *Milton: The Critical Heritage* (London, 1970).
Thorpe, James (ed.), *Milton Criticism* (London, 1965).

Thematic approaches
Bell, M., 'The Fallacy of the Fall in *Paradise Lost*', *PMLA* 68(1953), pp. 863–83.
Boyette, P. E., 'Something More About the Erotic Motive in *Paradise Lost*', *Tulane Studies in English* XV (1967), pp. 19–30.
Burden, D., *The Logical Epic* (London, 1967).
Christopher, G. B., *Milton and the Science of the Saints* (Princeton, NJ, 1982).
Danielson, D. R., *Milton's Good God* (Cambridge, 1982).
Dobbins, A. C., *Milton and the Book of Revelation* (Alabama, 1975).
Empson, W., *Milton's God* (London, 1961).
Evans, J. M., *'Paradise Lost' and the Genesis Tradition* (Oxford, 1968).
Freeman, J., *Milton and the Martial Muse* (Princeton, NJ, 1981).
Greenlaw, E., 'A Better Teacher Than Aquinas', *Studies in Philology* 14 (1917), pp. 196–217.
Halkett, J., *Milton and the Idea of Matrimony* (New Haven and London, 1970).
Haller, W., 'Hail Wedded Love', in *Rudrum, pp. 296–312.
Hanford, J. H., *John Milton: Poet and Humanist* (Cleveland, 1966).
Henson, L. D., 'The Witch in Eve: Milton's Use of Witchcraft in *Paradise Lost*', in *Franson, pp. 122–34.
Hoopes, R., *Right Reason in the English Renaissance* (Cambridge, Mass., and London, 1962).
Hunter, W. B., *et al.*, *Bright Essence: Studies in Milton's Theology* (Salt Lake City, 1971).
Kelley, M., *This Great Argument* (Princeton, NJ, 1941).
Kerrigan, W., *The Prophetic Milton* (Charlottesville, 1974).
Lewalski, B. K., 'Innocence and Experience in Milton's Eden', in *Kranidas, pp. 86–117.
Lewis, C. S., *A Preface to 'Paradise Lost'* (London, 1942).

Lindenbaum, P., 'Lovemaking in Milton's Paradise', *Milton Studies* 6 (1974), 277–306.

Lovejoy, A. O., 'Milton and the Paradox of the Fortunate Fall', *Journal of English Literary History* 4 (1937) pp. 161–79.

Madsen, W. G., *From Shadowy Types to Truth* (New Haven, Conn., and London, 1968).

Mahood, M. M., *Poetry and Humanism* (London, 1950).

Marshall, W. H., '*Paradise Lost: Felix Culpa* and the Problem of Structure', in *Barker, pp. 336–41.

Martz, L. L., *Poet of Exile* (New Haven and London, 1980).

Patrides, C. A., *Milton and the Christian Tradition* (Oxford, 1966).

——, ' "Something like Prophetic Strain" ', in Patrides and Wittreich, J. A. (ed.), *The Apocalypse in English Renaissance Thought and Literature* (Manchester, 1984), pp. 207–37.

Peter, J., *A Critique of 'Paradise Lost'* (London and New York, 1960).

Riggs, W. C., *The Christian Poet in 'Paradise Lost'* (Berkeley and London, 1972).

Ryken, L., *The Apocalyptic Vision in 'Paradise Lost'* (Ithaca, NY, and London, 1970).

Schultz, H., *Milton and Forbidden Knowledge* (New York and London, 1955).

Summers, J. H., *The Muse's Method* (Cambridge, Mass., 1962).

Svendsen, K., *Milton and Science* (Cambridge, Mass., and London, 1956).

Taylor, D., 'Milton and the Paradox of the Fortunate Fall Once More', *Tulane Studies in English* 9 (1959), pp. 35–52.

Tillyard, E. M. W., *Milton* (London, 1930).

Waddington, R., 'Appearance and Reality in Satan's Disguises', *Texas Studies in Language & Literature* 4 (1962), pp. 390–8.

Waldock, A. J. A., *'Paradise Lost' and Its Critics* (Cambridge, 1947).

Willey, B., *The Seventeenth-century Background* (1934; repr. Harmondsworth, 1962).

Form and genre

Barker, A. C., 'Structural Pattern in *Paradise Lost*', in *Barker, pp. 142–55.

Bowra, C. M., *From Virgil to Milton* (London, 1945).

Demaray, J. G., *Milton's Theatrical Epic* (Cambridge, Mass., and London, 1980).

Ferry, A. D., *Milton's Epic Voice* (Cambridge, Mass., 1963).

Frye, R. M., *Milton's Imagery and the Visual Arts* (Princeton, NJ, 1978).

Gardner, H., 'Milton's Satan and the Theme of Damnation in Elizabethan Tragedy', in *Barker, pp. 205–17.

Giamatti, A. B., *The Earthly Paradise and the Renaissance Epic* (Princeton, NJ, 1966).

Greene, T., *The Descent from Heaven* (New Haven and London, 1963).

Guillory, J., *Poetic Authority* (New York, 1983).

Hagin, P., *The Epic Hero and the Decline of Heroic Poetry* (Bern, 1964).

Harding, D. P., *The Club of Hercules* (Urbana, Ill., 1962).

Helgerson, R., *Self-Crowned Laureates* (Berkeley and London, 1983).

Kates, J. A., 'The Revaluation of the Classical Heroic in Tasso and Milton', *Comparative Literature* 26 (1974), pp. 299–317.

Knott, J. R., *Milton's Pastoral Vision* (Chicago, 1971).

Kurth, B. O., *Milton and Christian Heroism* (1959: repr. Hamden, Conn., 1966).

Lewalski, B. K., *'Paradise Lost' and the Rhetoric of Literary Forms* (Princeton, NJ, 1985).

——, 'The Genres of *Paradise Lost:* Literary Genre as a Means of Accommodation', *Milton Studies* 17 (1983) pp. 75–105.

Lieb, M., *Poetics of the Holy* (Chapel Hill, 1981).

Low, A., *The Georgic Revolution* (Princeton, NJ, 1985).

Nuttall, A. D., *Overheard by God* (London and New York, 1980).

Rosenblatt, J. P., 'Structural Unity and Temporal Concordance: the War in Heaven in *Paradise Lost*', *PMLA* 87 (1972), pp. 31–41.

Sasek, L. A., 'The Drama of *Paradise Lost*, Books XI and XII', in *Barker, pp. 342–56.

Schindler, W., *Voice and Crisis* (Hamden, Conn., 1984).

Shawcross, J. T., 'The Metaphor of Inspiration in *Paradise Lost*, in *Fiore, pp. 75–83.

——, 'The Balanced Structure of *Paradise Lost*', *Studies in Philology* 62 (1965) pp. 696–718.

Sims, J. H., and Ryken, L., *Milton and Scriptural Tradition* (Columbia, Miss., 1984).

Spencer, T. J. B., *'Paradise Lost:* The Anti-Epic', in *Patrides, pp. 81–98.

Steadman, J. M., *Milton and the Renaissance Hero* (Oxford, 1967).

——, *Milton's Epic Characters* (Chapel Hill, 1968).

Stein, A., *Answerable Style* (Minneapolis and London, 1953).

Stevenson, K., ' "No More . . . No End"; *Paradise Lost* IX', *Renaissance Papers* (1984), pp. 103–9.

Toliver, H. E., 'Milton's Household Epic', *Milton Studies* 9 (1976), pp. 105–20.

Webber, J., *Milton and His Epic Tradition* (Seattle, 1979).
Wittreich, J. A., *Visionary Poetics* (San Marino, Calif., 1979).

Historical approaches
Bennett, J. S., 'God, Satan, and King Charles: Milton's Royal Portraits', *PMLA* 92 (1977), pp. 441–57.
Berry, B. M., *Process of Speech* (Baltimore and London, 1976).
Davies, S., *Images of Kingship in 'Paradise Lost'* (Columbia, Miss., 1983).
Fallon, R. T., *Captain or Colonel* (Columbia, Miss., 1984).
Firth, K. R., *The Apocalyptic Tradition in Reformation Britain, 1530–1645* (Oxford, 1979).
Fixler, M., *Milton and the Kingdoms of God* (London, 1964).
Hill, C., *Milton and the English Revolution* (London, 1977).
Hodge, B., 'Satan and the Revolution of the Saints', in Aers, D. *et al.* (ed.), *Literature, Language and Society in England, 1580–1680* (Totowa, NJ, 1981), pp. 184–99.
Milner, A., *John Milton and the English Revolution* (London, 1981).
Revard, S. P., *The War in Heaven* (Ithaca, NY, and London, 1980).
Ross, M., *Milton and Royalism* (Ithaca, NY, 1943).
Stocker, M., *Apocalyptic Marvell* (Brighton, 1986).
Whiting, G. W., *Milton's Literary Milieu* (New York, 1964).

Psychology and myth
Bergonzi, B., 'Criticism and the Milton Controversy', in *Kermode, pp. 162–80.
Bloom, H., *The Anxiety of Influence* (New York, 1973).
Bodkin, M., *Archetypal Patterns in Poetry* (London, 1934).
Cope, J. I., *The Metaphoric Structure of 'Paradise Lost'* (Baltimore, 1962).
Diekhoff, J. S. (ed.), *Milton on Himself* (New York and London, 1939).
Duncan, J. E., 'Archetypes in Milton's Earthly Paradise', *Milton Studies* 14 (1980), pp. 25–57.
Frye, N., *The Anatomy of Criticism* (London, 1957).
——, 'The Revelation to Eve', in *Rajan, pp. 18–47.
Kermode, F., 'Adam Unparadised', in *Kermode, pp. 85–123.
Kerrigan, W., *The Sacred Complex* (Cambridge, Mass., and London, 1983).
Le Comte, E., *Milton and Sex* (London, 1978).
——, *Milton's Unchanging Mind* (Port Washington, NY, 1973).
——, 'Miltonic Echoes in *Elegia VII*', *English Literary Renaissance* 14 (1984), pp. 191–8.

Lentricchia, F., *After the New Criticism* (London, 1980).
MacCaffrey, I. G., *'Paradise Lost' as "Myth"* (Cambridge, Mass., 1959).
Rudat, W., 'Milton, Freud, St. Augustine: *Paradise Lost* and the History of Human Sexuality', *Mosaic* 15 (1982), pp. 109–121.
Shawcross, J. T., *With Mortal Voice* (Lexington, KY, 1982).
Tayler, E. W., *Milton's Poetry: Its Development in Time* (Pittsburgh, 1979).
Weber, B. J., 'The Non-Narrative Approaches to *Paradise Lost:* A Gentle Remonstrance', *Milton Studies* 9 (1976), pp. 77–103.
Werblowsky, R. J. Z., 'Antagonist of Heaven's Almighty King', in *Dyson, pp. 129–51.

Reader and text
Bouchard, D. F., *Milton: a structural reading* (London, 1974).
Crosman, R., *Reading 'Paradise Lost'* (Bloomington, 1980).
Culler, J. *Structuralist Poetics* (London, 1975).
Fish, S., *Is There a Text in This Class?* (Cambridge, Mass., 1980).
——, *Surprised by Sin* (London and New York, 1967).
Foucault, M., 'What Is an Author?', in *The Foucault Reader*, ed. P. Rabinow (Harmondsworth, 1986).
Hartman, G., 'Milton's Counterplot', in *Barker, pp. 386–97.
Jauss, H. R., 'Literary History as a Challenge to Literary Theory', in *Toward an Aesthetic of Reception* (Brighton, 1982), pp. 3–45.
Kendrick, C., *Milton: A Study in Ideology and Form* (New York and London, 1986).
Knott, J. R., *'Paradise Lost* and the Fit Reader', *Modern Language Quarterly* 45 (1984) pp. 123–43.
Nyquist, M., 'Reading the Fall: Discourse in Drama in *Paradise Lost*', *English Literary Renaissance* 14 (1984) pp. 199–229.
Parker, P., *Inescapable Romance* (Princeton, NJ, 1979).
Prince, G., 'Introduction to the Study of the Narratee', in *Reader-Response Criticism: From Formalism to Post-Structuralism*, ed. Jane P. Tompkins (Baltimore and London, 1980), pp. 7–25.
Rajan, B., *'Paradise Lost' and the Seventeenth-century Reader* (London, 1947).
Rapaport, H., *Milton and the Postmodern* (Lincoln, Neb., and London, 1983).
Stocker, M., 'God in Theory: Milton, Literature and Theodicy', *Journal of Literature & Theology* I (1987), pp. 70–88.
Wheeler, T., *'Paradise Lost' and the Modern Reader* (Athens, GA, 1974).

Wimsatt, W. K., 'The Intentional Fallacy', in *The Verbal Icon* (Lexington, 1954).

Feminist approaches

Aers, D. and Hodge, B., ' "Rational Burning": Milton on Sex and Marriage', in Aers *et al.* (ed.), *Literature, Language and Society* (Totowa, NJ, 1981).

Anderson, D., 'Unfallen Marriage and the Fallen Imagination in *Paradise Lost*', *Studies in English Literature* 26 (1986), pp. 125–44.

Davies, S., *The Idea of Woman in Renaissance Literature* (Brighton, 1986).

DiSalvo, J., 'Blake Encountering Milton: Politics and the Family in *Paradise Lost* and *The Four Zoas*', in Wittreich, Joseph (ed.), *Milton and the Line of Vision* (Madison, Wis., 1975), 143–84; cf. DiSalvo, *War of Titans* (Pittsburgh, 1983).

Farwell, M., 'Eve, the Separation Scene, and the Renaissance Idea of Androgyny', *Milton Studies* 16 (1982), pp. 3–20.

Froula, C., 'When Eve reads Milton: Undoing the Canonical Economy', *Critical Inquiry* 10 (1983), pp. 321–47; argument with E. Pechter, *CI* 11 (1984), pp. 163–78.

Gilbert, S., 'Patriarchal Poetry and Women Readers: Reflections on Milton's Bogey', *PMLA* 93 (1978), pp. 368–82; repr. in Gilbert and S. Gubar, *The Madwoman in the Attic* (New Haven and London, 1979), pp. 187–212.

Graves, R., *Wife to Mr Milton* (1942: repr. Harmondsworth, 1954).

Landy, M., 'Kinship and the Role of Women in *Paradise Lost*', *Milton Studies* 4 (1972), pp. 3–18.

——, ' "A Free and Open Encounter": Milton and the Modern Reader', *Milton Studies* 9 (1976), pp. 3–36.

Lewalski, B. K., 'Milton on Women – Yet Once More', *Milton Studies* 6 (1974) pp. 3–20.

McColley, D. K., *Milton's Eve* (Urbana and London, 1983).

Moi, T., *Sexual/Textual Politics* (London and New York, 1985).

Mollenkott, V., 'Some Implications of Milton's Androgynous Muse', *Bucknell Review* 24 (1978), pp. 27–36.

Quilligan, M., *Milton's Spenser* (Ithaca and London, 1983).

Revard, S. P., 'Eve and the Doctrine of Responsibility in *Paradise Lost*', *PMLA* 88 (1973) pp. 69–78.

Rogers, K. M., *The Troublesome Helpmate* (Seattle and London, 1966).

Safer, E. B., ' "Sufficient to Have Stood": Eve's Responsibility in Book IX', *Milton Quarterly* 6 (1972), pp. 10–14.

Webber, J. M., 'The Politics of Poetry: Feminism and *Paradise Lost*', *Milton Studies* 14 (1980), pp. 3–24.

Guide to further study
Theme: Summers, J. H., *The Muse's Method* (Cambridge, Mass., 1962).
Style: Ricks, C., *Milton's Grand Style* (London and New York, 1963).
Historical: Fixler, M., *Milton and the Kingdoms of God* (London, 1964).
Marxist: Hill, C., *Milton and the English Revolution* (London, 1977).
    Milner, A., *John Milton and the English Revolution* (London, 1981).
Mythic: Frye, N., 'The Revelation to Eve', in *Rajan, pp. 18–47.
Psychoanalytic: Kerrigan, W., *The Sacred Complex* (Cambridge, Mass., and London, 1983).
Reader-response: Fish, S., *Surprised by Sin* (London and New York, 1967).
Deconstructive: Hartman, G., 'Adam on the Grass with Balsamum', in *Beyond Formalism* (New Haven and London, 1970), pp. 124–50.
Feminist: McColley, Diane K., *Milton's Eve* (Urbana and London, 1983).

Index to Critics

Kermode, F.   10, 14, 36, 86, 90
Kerrigan, W.   42, 75, 87, 90, 93
Knott, J. R.   23, 26, 61, 89, 91
Kurth, B. O.   25, 89

Landy, M.   50, 53–4, 92
Leavis, F. R.   13, 86
Le Comte, E.   41, 42, 52, 90
Lentricchia, F.   37, 42, 91
Lewalski, B. K.   22, 26–7, 45, 53, 54, 55, 87, 89, 92
Lewis, C. S.   13, 15, 20, 22, 23, 24, 47, 87
Lieb, M.   75, 89
Lindenbaum, P.   51, 88
Lovejoy, A. O.   20, 88
Lovelock, J.   14, 86
Low, A.   26, 89

MacCaffrey, I. G.   39–40, 41, 91
Madsen, W. G.   31–2, 33, 88
Mahood, M. M.   15, 88
Marshall, W. H.   20, 88
Martz, L. L.   41, 88
McColley, D. K.   55–6, 58, 92, 93
Milner, A.   33–4, 90, 93
Moi, T.   57, 92
Mollenkott, V.   57, 92
Murray, P.   13, 87

Nuttall, A. D.   73, 89
Nyquist, M.   48–9, 55, 91

Parker, P.   48, 91
Parker, W. R.   11, 87
Patrides, C. A.   18, 27, 86, 88
Peter, J.   31, 88
Prince, G.   67, 91

Quilligan, M.   52–3, 54, 56, 92

Rajan, B.   24, 27, 44, 86, 91
Raleigh, W.   12, 87
Rapaport, H.   47–8, 91

Revard, S. P.   35, 55, 90, 92
Ricks, C.   93
Riggs, W. C.   78, 88
Rogers, K. M.   52, 92
Rosenblatt, J. P.   41, 89
Ross, M.   31, 90
Rudat, W.   41–2, 91
Rudrum, A.   50, 86
Ryken, L.   25, 26, 27, 30, 45, 88, 89

Safer, E. B.   55, 92
Samuel, I.   10, 14, 45, 87
Sasek, L. A.   29, 89
Saurat, D.   12, 87
Schindler, W.   30, 89
Schultz, H.   17, 88
Shawcross, J. T.   32, 41, 57, 87, 89, 91
Sims, J. H.   25, 27, 30, 89
Spencer, T. J. B.   25, 89
Steadman, J. M.   23, 24, 89
Stein, A.   28, 31, 89
Stevenson, K.   29, 89
Stocker, M.   21, 61, 90, 91
Summers, J. H.   32, 88, 93
Svendsen, K.   17, 88

Tayler, E. W.   42, 91
Thorpe, J.   11, 87
Tillyard, E. M. W.   12, 14, 15, 19, 50, 52, 54, 88
Toliver, H. E.   51, 89

Waddington, R., 29, 88
Waldock, A. J. A.   13, 19, 21, 24, 30, 33, 37, 43, 88
Webber, J.   25, 27, 57, 58, 90, 93
Weber, B. J.   39, 40, 43–4, 91
Weblowsky, R. J. Z.   40–1, 91
Wheeler, T.   45, 91
Whiting, G. W.   31, 90
Willey, B.   17, 21, 88
Wimsatt, W. K.   14, 91
Wittreich J. A.   27, 90